'An exciting story of being a missionary today in four African countries, Liz Parker, a mum, teacher, and wife of an MAF pilot, gives an honest and humorous account of living daily by faith, including her family's gripping escape from civil war in South Sudan. I highly recommend this book.'

John Butterworth, MBE, author, newspaper editor and journalist

'This is an inspiring and honest account of challenges courageously faced on the mission field. Liz reveals her grappling with questions about God's care as she encountered life-threatening situations. Yet fun, laughter and her love for Africa shine through. She discovers God is greater than war, trauma, fears and failures. I couldn't put it down.'

Charles Marnham, Former Vicar, St Michael's Chester Square, London

'I am profoundly inspired and impressed by this very powerful book. Liz Parker has written a deeply moving, interesting and compelling book. I especially value the accounts of MAF's Ministry and the poignant details of the situations of the people they reach. This book is so well written it is very hard to put down! I strongly recommend it as a "must read" book.'

The Baroness Cox, Founder and CEO, Humanitarian Aid Relief Trust

'We are immensely privileged that so many people like Liz and the Parker family commit their lives to fulfil the mission of MAF. But it is rare to get such an in-depth and heartfelt insight into what life is really like on the mission field. This book gives examples of the miraculous victories, inspiring faith and daily provision that God provides to those who choose to follow Him.'

Ruth Whitaker, CEO, MAF UK

Immeasurably More

LIZ PARKER

FLYING FOR THE WAY-MAKER

Immeasurably More

LIZ PARKER

10 Publishing

Copyright © 2021 by Liz Parker

First published in Great Britain in 2021

British Library Cataloguing in Publication Data
A record for this book is available from the British Library

ISBN: 978-1-913896-15-7

Designed and typeset by Pete Barnsley (CreativeHoot.com)

Printed in Denmark by Nørhaven

10Publishing, a division of 10ofthose.com
Unit C, Tomlinson Road, Leyland, PR25 2DY, England

Email: info@10ofthose.com
Website: www.10ofthose.com

1 3 5 7 10 8 6 4 2

For my mum – my inspiration,
and very great friend

Let this be written for a future generation,
*that a people not yet created may praise the L*ORD.
(Psalm 102:18)

Contents

PART FIVE: SOUTH SUDAN (AUGUST 2014 – JULY 2016)

PART SIX: UGANDA (DECEMBER 2016 ONWARDS)

Prologue:

SOUTH SUDAN, 8 JULY 2016

Bang! Bang! The sounds of heavy gunfire ripped the air apart. Each new volley of shots made me jump. My legs were shaking, but I was determined not to let my fear show. I plastered on a smile and turned to my children. I was grateful for my long trousers – hopefully they couldn't see how my limbs had turned to jelly.

The gunfire continued, loud 'pops' interspersed with booming undertones. From the street came the sounds of rubber soles hitting the paving at speed – local people running, trying to get to safety. No one wanted to be caught in the crossfire. The ground shook as another armoured vehicle sped past on the road outside. Just a low wall and a leafy, green hedge separated us from the menace on the streets of Juba, the capital city, that evening. *Leaves don't offer much protection*, I thought, as I scanned the outside yard of Quality Hotel where we were gathered.

Across the yard, I caught my husband's eye. Normally laid-back and relaxed, Andrew's expression was anxious, worry creasing his eyes. This was supposed to be a pizza night with friends and colleagues at our favourite local restaurant. Our food had already been ordered when the distinct sounds of gunfire shockingly interrupted our conversation. We were a large party of fourteen adults and thirteen children, but before we could make a collective decision about whether the first gunshots were serious, the security guard at the entrance to the hotel locked the doors. Now we had no choice but to stay within the confines of the hotel – and who knew how long we would have to remain there?

A longer burst of gunfire spurred us into action.

'Get the children to safety!' someone yelled.

Parents started to round them up. I herded my three children – ten-year-old Esther, eight-year-old Ben and five-year-old Joel – into the hotel's bar, the first building that opened on to the yard. We began to line the children up along the brick wall, but the bricks each had a decorative hole right through their centre. *This is not going to prevent bullets hitting them,* I thought in distress.

Someone must have had a similar idea because, a few minutes later, a tense staff member in white uniform ushered us into the bathroom. Hot, flustered and confused, we tried to fit into the small space, but it simply wasn't big enough. The next thing I knew, hotel staff were fumbling with keys and managed to open a door leading to an inner courtyard. Our party surged through to an enclosed area. At least here we had the protection of solid walls.

It felt like hours, although in reality it was just over one hour, while guns blazed less than two kilometres across town – the occasional shot erupting much closer. Fear was tangible, but so was the determination of the parents to stay calm for their children. I stood near my good friend Nathalie, while Esther and Ben sat at our feet with her children – their friends – on the cool paving stones of the courtyard.

'When's our pizza coming?' enquired hungry children. There was no answer. The chef had stopped cooking as soon as the gunshots began. The people of Juba are sadly too familiar with the deafening sounds of hatred. Gunfire halts normality.

Over by the wall, Andrew stood among the other men of our party, their faces serious as they discussed possible plans to get us to safety. Joel stood close to Andrew, the man he felt safe with, his blond head tilted as he looked up at his dad. 'But we'll be all right, won't we, Daddy?' he asked, his blue eyes full of concern.

Andrew couldn't answer and that hurt his heart. We had no idea how this would turn out – how could he give his son honest reassurance when echoes of danger filled our ears?

What we did know is that God had never let us down – so we prayed urgently for His protection, confident that He could hear us above the gunshots.

Part One

Where it all began

1967 - 2004

1
A legacy of love for Africa

The confidence underlying my prayers on that South Sudan day didn't come from me alone. It was inspired by the generation before me.

Stories of God's help and protection, His faithfulness and guidance had been passed to me from my earliest days. Tales were told and photos shown of when our family first forged links with Africa – before my birth. Now I was the one standing on African soil, praying urgent prayers to the same God who took my mum, Ann, from London to Uganda in the mid-sixties. Just as my mother had done before me, we would see God's faithfulness, even in those terrifying moments when I stood with my children, listening to the threat of civil war in a country that was not my own.

My mum's calling was different from mine, but in time our stories were beautifully woven together, in ways we never imagined. Her calling was to work as a teacher in Karamoja – those vast, wild grasslands of north-eastern Uganda. A land where the savannah stretched as far as the eye could see, where the light of the relentless sun lent a gilded quality to the sandy earth. The occasional thorn tree and a scrub of bushes punctuated this seemingly endless landscape. Heat shimmered over the baked earth, dry dust settled on the land.

It was an unexpected calling. My mum had a British friend, Sylvia, who suggested that Mum join her as a teacher at a new girl's school in Kotido, a small settlement of Karamoja in Uganda. Sylvia needed a British colleague to work alongside her in this remote region and felt that God was calling Ann to be that person. 'Kotido?' my mum asked. 'I don't even know where Uganda is, never mind Kotido!' Sceptical, Mum wrote by airmail to tell Sylvia that she would not be coming.

Sylvia, however, was convinced that God wanted my mum for the job. 'Have you prayed about it, Ann?' her next letter asked.

'I suppose I could pray about it,' thought Mum, and she did exactly that. The more she prayed, the more she started to wonder whether Sylvia was right. Cycling across town one day, she was incredulous when a billboard caught her eye. It was advertising a documentary to be shown at the local cinema: *Karamoja, Land of Naked People*. It was simply too amazing to be a coincidence. From then on, my mum felt like she had received confirmation of God calling her to far-off Uganda and, specifically, to Karamoja.

Mum took my grandmother with her to watch this one-off film, which neither of them ever heard about again. As they settled into their seats, Mum was fascinated by the black-and-white documentary, which demonstrated the time-honoured traditions of a fierce warrior tribe of pastoralists. They were a people steeped in a culture totally different to her own. The naked men and children, the women wearing only animal skins, the cattle raids, the thatched homes woven from wood and mud: each image evoked a world apart. At the end of the film, my grandmother turned to my mum, shocked by such an unfamiliar lifestyle. 'Ann, you are *NOT* going there!' she exclaimed.

But Ann *did* go, setting off in August 1967, convinced of God's call to teach in the Kotido school. My grandmother recognised my mum's unshakable conviction – and decided to give her daughter her unwavering support. As Mum embarked on her first flight from London to Uganda, her trust was founded on words she had read in the book of Isaiah: 'you are precious and honoured in my sight, and because I love you... Do not be afraid, for I am with you... I, even I, am the LORD, and apart from me there is no saviour' (Isaiah 43:4, 5, 11). These words of promise also gave her the desire to share the news of this Saviour with her students in sun-scorched, remote Kotido.

As a child, I loved to turn the pages of Mum's hard-backed photo album and enter into this African world, which was a million miles and a generation away from our Liverpool vicarage. It couldn't be more different from the built-up city outside our windows, where factories, apartment blocks and tight terraced streets hemmed us in. Where inclement British weather cast shadows on the concrete and where the climate could hardly be described as hot.

Even better than the photo albums were the slideshows Mum organised. She invited members of our Bootle church to come and hear her testimony of God's faithfulness, to learn about a still-neglected area of Uganda and to pray for a people she continued to hold dear to her heart. Mum left these people in 1969, when she returned home to England to marry my dad, David. She was heartbroken saying goodbye to her beloved students and her beloved Karamoja, believing she would never see either again, but at least she could tell us about them.

I sat spellbound on the carpet of our vicarage lounge as black-and-white scenes from Kotido flashed up on a huge screen. My dad, the local vicar, helpfully operated the old-fashioned projector, which whirred noisily in the background, while my mum's voice rose to explain each image. Men and women from St Leonard's Church sat attentive on their chairs, watching 1960s Uganda come to life in 1980s Liverpool.

First of all, the photographs transported us to Kotido Girl's School, where my mum worked as one of four teachers. We saw her students, their broad smiles reflecting hope as education opened its welcoming door. Mum described how much she enjoyed teaching these girls with their keen minds and energy. She spoke of their beautiful, traditional singing.

There were challenges – she related sadly how Monica, a sweet girl with a sweet smile, failed to return to school one term after being forced into a polygamous marriage to an older tribal chief. Mum regretted how choice had been stripped away from Monica. For other girls, though, getting an education gave them options beyond tradition. We heard about Okia, one of her brightest students and after whom my earliest doll had been named. Mum's passion for education shone through.

We gazed in wonder at Karamojong warriors, standing lithe and proud, adorned with colourful beads, metal armbands and astonishing lip-plugs. We learnt that Karamojong family groups lived in *manyatta*, a cluster of round, thatch homes, enclosed within a woven thorn fence. Mum described how she had to crawl in through a small gap – the entrance was designed this way to keep out threats. Goats, dogs and chickens made up part of the lively community within each *manyatta*, but most important of all were the cattle. For this tribe of pastoralists, cattle were wealth.

Mum introduced us to Rachel, an older lady wreathed in wrinkles. Rachel grinned at the camera, revealing gaps where teeth were missing, confidently at ease with my mum as she snapped the photograph. Rachel's clothing was the simple hide of a cow wrapped around her waist, with a blanket loosely knotted across her bare breasts and hanging off her shoulders. We were sorry to hear how, in a place without doctors, her young son died of meningitis. The only treatment had been a traditional one: a long gash cut across his forehead 'to allow the evil spirits out'.

Another image depicted a group of children, some kneeling, some sitting with their legs outstretched on the brittle, parched grass. Most wore nothing except a string or two of beads around their neck and metal bands around their ankles. Some wore loincloths. Nearly all had distended bellies, a sign of malnutrition in a region prone to drought and failed crops. Happy smiles, though, showed their enjoyment of their weekly Sunday School class, held under the shade of a tamarind tree. Some of Mum's students held the class in Karamojong, a language my mum never mastered. 'The one song I learnt clearly in Karamojong was, "Zacchaeus was a very little man" – and I can still sing it today!' Mum laughed. It was a story of a man who found peace and friendship with Jesus – something Mum prayed her Sunday School class, her students and her village friends would find.

We heard how God protected my mum from an unscrupulous fellow traveller. Early one morning, as the pale dawn sun slipped effortlessly into the African sky, she boarded the bus from Moroto to Kotido, a route which passed through wild, forsaken bush. There was one other passenger – and he sat right beside her, the young, single foreigner. The man became threatening, placing his hand on her knee. Too close for comfort, he leaned in to inform her that she would become his wife, but that if she didn't agree to do as he wished, he would throw her off the bus, leaving her alone and unprotected, prey for wild animals: a very real threat. Afraid and vulnerable, Ann sent up a prayer for help. Suddenly inspired, she declared, 'I am the daughter of a King! God is watching over me. There will be serious consequences if anything happens to me.'

Her unwelcome companion raised his eyebrows in surprise, but stubbornly continued his threats – until the bus suddenly pulled over. Another man climbed aboard. To Ann's immense surprise and relief, she recognised the new passenger. He was a teacher from Kotido Boy's School, with whom she sometimes worked. Ann enthusiastically greeted her Ugandan colleague and her aggressor got up and left her in peace. She was no longer easy prey for his ill intentions.

It was good to hear that my mum safely reached her home that day, but she was still shaken by the ordeal. However, feelings of peace washed over her when she read with astonishment the Bible passage recommended for that specific day by her daily devotional. Her eyes fell on these beautifully relevant words: 'pray that we may be delivered from wicked and evil people… the Lord is faithful, and he will strengthen you and protect you from the evil one' (2 Thessalonians 3:2–3). Reassurance wrapped its kindly arms around her. She had just experienced this exact truth.

Decades later, we listened as my mum related this story to encourage us. Difficulties may come, but God answers prayers, God protects His people in times of need, God's timing is perfection – these were the truths she passed on. Those faith lessons stayed with me right into – and out of – South Sudan.

Each story she told, each image I saw stirred in me a passion for adventure in faraway lands, confident that God would go with me. As a teenager, I made my own commitment to follow Jesus, this faithful One who cares for all people, in all nations. This was the start of my own unique journey, as our God took me out of Liverpool and into Africa, and proved that He is greater than all we might ask or imagine.

2

Mr Right and a wild promise

Mine was a fun, lively, Liverpudlian childhood. Like all childhoods, it flew by. I grew up alongside my brothers, Stephen and Ian, in an enormous vicarage in Bootle, Merseyside. Our home was constantly buzzing with people. Sometimes it felt like I was growing up in a busy train station because there were so many visitors passing through our doors, but it was very welcoming, filled with love and laughter. The vicarage itself – an ancient, rambling house, with creaky staircases that linked its three storeys – was full-brimmed with adventure. The top floor boasted a self-contained flat with windows cut into the eaves, offering views over the industrial docks and the choppy waters of the River Mersey.

This top-floor flat was significant in beckoning me further towards foreign adventures since many missionaries came to stay there, some of them for months at a time, while they studied at the Liverpool School of Tropical Medicine. These committed, talented people from Europe or America inspired me with their stories of tropical destinations, and with their passionate desire to share their faith and use their medical gifts to serve strangers in unknown countries. With every passing year, the pull for me to go overseas grew stronger. By the time I left home at eighteen, I was more than ready to spread my wings, to discover more of our vast and exciting world, to search for my own calling.

At first, I ventured closer to home. I studied French at Nottingham University and, as part of my course, spent a fantastic year in France. Next, I studied to become a teacher. My first teaching job was in London's Westminster borough, at St Saviour's Primary School: a job I loved. Since I now earned money to pay for adventures overseas, I contacted my friend Su-Pin and spent my summer holiday visiting her Singaporean home. This colourful taste of life in the Far East spurred me on to explore more of the world.

Eighteen months after this trip, I gave up my job and moved to South Africa to work as a volunteer for the Christian charity Scripture Union. After six months in Cape Town, I boarded a flight out of Johannesburg and set off on a year-long trek around the world, with several months in Sydney, Australia. Here, I worked as a supply teacher for an agency and shared a flat with two good friends from my London church – one of whom was a handsome, blond, blue-eyed South African named Andrew. His sense of humour, his easy acceptance of people and his love of adventure made him a happy companion. Over time, our friendship grew, though neither of us realised then how significant it would become.

On my return to London, I began a new teaching job in Bethnal Green, at St Paul with St Luke's Primary School. During this season, I found that many friends had moved on to a new chapter in their lives: marriage. Still single, I relished my freedom – but had high hopes of romance. I began to pray very specifically about meeting Mr Right. One day, I blurted out a wild promise to the Lord: 'I'll go anywhere for you, if only you'll give me someone to go with!' I was soon to learn that God takes us at our word...

It was just over a year later that Andrew returned to London from a temporary office job in Christchurch, New Zealand. I excitedly welcomed my good friend back to London. One chilly, winter afternoon, he and I set off for a walk along the blustery towpath of the River Thames at Fulham. Stopping for a plate of chips at a riverside pub, Andrew's tone suddenly became serious. 'Liz, I know you're close to your family,' he began, 'but could you see yourself living overseas?'

I paused, startled by his question.

'Yes, I definitely could,' was my reply. What was he implying? I was intrigued.

Just a few weeks later, Andrew surprised me again with his suggestion that perhaps we could be more than good friends?

Eleven months later, in December 2003, I stood proudly with Andrew at the front of our London church – St Michael's, Chester Square – and happily promised to be his wife. It was a joy-filled, jazz-filled, candlelit wedding, just a few days before Christmas. As the last notes of the jazz band faded away, we set off in a black London cab – as Mr and Mrs Parker.

God had given me someone wonderful with whom to share my life. Like me, Andrew was crafted by God with an internal pull overseas. Now would I follow through and literally go 'anywhere' for God?

One evening, a few months after our marriage, a visiting speaker came to St Michael's church service. It was an evening where Andrew was busy helping out in another part of the church – out of my sight – while I sat elsewhere with friends.

The talk was based on Isaiah 6:8: 'Then I heard the voice of the LORD saying, "Whom shall I send? And who will go for us?"' The words made my stomach flip; I experienced an inexplicable, irresistible Holy Spirit prompting, entreating me to respond with the second part of the verse, 'And I said, "Here am I. Send me!"' The speaker invited those who felt a call to serve God, wherever He may call us, to come forward for prayer. Then the worship band took up their instruments to play the next song, whose lyrics were taken directly from this verse in Isaiah. I found the words compelling, but I couldn't sing them. I had to act on them.

As the notes rang out and the congregation's voices began to rise, I found that I too rose – to walk to the front for prayer, with a strong conviction in my heart. I would go, if God would lead the way.

I was astonished, on reaching the front of the church, to find Andrew already standing there. I had promised God to 'go anywhere' – and now discovered that my husband felt the same!

God's promise, though, was greater than ours. We agreed to go, but He promised to lead. Even if God called us to places we knew little about, to a job we never envisaged, we would only move forward because He made a way.

3

A letter from God?

Andrew and I were full of anticipation. It had been exciting to find each other at the front of church that evening, to stand on the brink of a new journey together. Now we needed directions.

Life had become routine. I enjoyed teaching at the new job I had taken at Hill House School, when I moved across London to marry Andrew. Andrew enjoyed his job as general assistant at St Michael's, our lively, friendly, central London church. He got on well with the office team and our wonderful vicar, Charles Marnham. But something was starting to change. A restlessness was stirring. Andrew was looking ahead, searching for something long-term after years of temporary jobs. Now he was searching for a career: one where He could serve God, but not necessarily in a church setting.

We decided we needed to pray very specifically, so began to ask God to show us where He wanted us to go and which job would be right for Andrew. For several months we prayed, without any indication of what might be next.

It was through our letterbox that an answer came.

Andrew came home from work and stooped to pick up our post, which had dropped silently on to the hallway carpet. As he checked the pile of friendly letters and not-so-friendly bills, his eye fell on a cellophane-wrapped magazine. 'Flying for Life' its title announced, while a photo of a light aircraft dominated the cover. He had never seen a magazine like this before. Scribbled pen obliterated the old student address at which I once lived and our new address had been clearly marked.

'What's this magazine?' he asked.

'Oh, that's a Christian charity I sometimes support: Mission Aviation Fellowship,' I replied. 'They have pilots who fly small planes into difficult places and carry goods like medicines, aid, church workers and evangelists.' I didn't tell Andrew how my flat-mate Rachel and I had admired the photos of the pilots in their smart uniforms!

Andrew opened the magazine – and was transfixed. He had never heard of a mission group using aeroplanes to share God's love in practical ways. He scrutinised the magazine, finding out as much as possible about their life-giving work.

A short while later, when Andrew arrived for work at St Michael's church office, his colleagues noticed something different. Andrew practically bounced down the steep stone steps and burst into their basement office. He definitely had an extra spring in his step.

Tina, a vivacious colleague and friend, glanced up from her desk. 'So, Andrew,' she ventured, 'have you decided yet what you're going to do with your life?'

'Yes,' Andrew smiled broadly. 'I'm going to go and fly planes for God in Africa.'

4

God only steers a moving ship

Having such an amazing idea was exciting – but was this a vision we could really pursue?

It seemed crazy. Andrew had no experience with flying. We knew nothing about the world of aviation and we still knew very little about the charity MAF (Mission Aviation Fellowship). We needed more information and we needed to pray.

When we discovered that basic pilot training cost around £40,000 in England, we gasped. We certainly couldn't afford to pay that. It cost almost half the amount for Andrew to train in his native South Africa, but even that was more than we had. Should we even consider such a wild idea?

The more we prayed about it, the more we were surprised by unexpected happenings. One day, Andrew received a phone call from a kind gentleman, a member of our church. 'Andrew,' Robin began, 'I know you are thinking about this missionary aviation idea. Well, I would like to pay for you to have a flight lesson. Just to see if you like it, you know. If you do, you can keep pressing on with the idea. What do you think?'

Andrew thought that Robin was the most generous of friends – and that it was a great idea. He set off early one morning to Biggin Hill, an airfield in Greater London, for his first proper flying lesson. Getting into that small plane and having the chance to handle the machine was brilliant: Andrew loved it. We thanked Robin profusely for his thoughtfulness.

We resolved not to tell others how much pilot training cost. Instead, we decided to ask God for the resources for Andrew's training – if this is where He was leading us, he would provide. We were still questioning whether it was feasible. I would need to resign from my teaching post and Andrew would be a full-time student. We would have no income. The application process for my South African visa was lengthy and until it was completed, I would not be permitted to earn a salary. This made me feel insecure. The flight training would consume our savings, so what would we live on?

We started to receive astonishing messages. One couple, good friends of ours, told us that they had prayed for us and decided they were going to deposit the tithe from their income (ten per cent) directly into our bank account for the duration of Andrew's pilot training. They were in the process of moving to a new house and therefore didn't currently have a church to which they were giving. A precious group of prayerful, caring ladies from St Leonard's Church, where I grew up in Bootle, wrote to say they wanted to give us a regular gift to help us move towards working with MAF. Another London friend told us that he was going to pay a monthly amount into our bank account if we moved to South Africa. We could barely believe all the kindness. God was causing others to catch the vision of Andrew flying for MAF – even if we still had doubts.

Around that time, we went away on a weekend retreat with our church community to Ashburnham Place in Sussex. I was to travel with a happy carload of friends and meet Andrew there. Andrew was tasked, along with a good friend of ours named Simon, with driving a van full of church equipment to the conference centre. Along the motorway, the two men became engrossed in a conversation about our potential move to South Africa for pilot training. Andrew admitted his fears and concerns to Simon. Even if he did become a pilot, Andrew reasoned, there was no certainty that MAF would have a place for him. 'Maybe it's easier to drop the idea and remain in England?' Andrew wondered.

Simon gave Andrew an answer that he couldn't forget: 'Andrew, God only steers a moving ship.'

The rest of the conversation is lost in the mists of time, but those words remained with Andrew. We couldn't just sit around and talk about flying for MAF. We had to actually *do* something about it.

The teaching theme of the weekend reinforced this. Looking at the incidence of David facing Goliath, the overriding message for us seemed to be, 'Face your fears. Be proactive. Step forward in faith, as David did, and trust that God will steer the way.'

We started to push ahead with plans – in early November 2004 we found ourselves on a flight to South Africa.

Part Two

South Africa
and England

NOVEMBER 2004 – NOVEMBER 2009

5

Amazing surprises

It was paradise. Stunning views spread out underneath our aeroplane window. White, sandy beaches curved around a green peninsula. The bright blue of the seas hugged the coastline. Everything was such striking refreshment for my eyes, accustomed to the dull grey of London in November.

Sunshine splashed across the vista below. It was such a cheerful welcome to South Africa. Yet my stomach was churning, anxious butterflies taking flight even while our plane was doing the opposite and descending towards Cape Town.

Not for the first time, I turned to my husband of eleven months, silently seeking reassurance. Were we doing the right thing? My heart told me yes, even though my head told me we must be crazy – but there was no going back. We were committed to Andrew's flight training. We stayed with a dear friend in Cape Town for a few days, bought a car and then drove it to Port Alfred to find a place to live. In just a couple of weeks, Andrew began his flight training at 43 Air School.

We discovered that Port Alfred was situated in a beautiful spot, with pristine beaches sloping into the vast blue of the Indian Ocean. Its marina boasted a multitude of merry boats, bobbing about on the lapping waves. This was a dream destination for holidaymakers.

But we were not holidaymakers. Learning to live in Port Alfred was a challenge for me. It was so different from London – my first real battle with culture shock. The quiet streets, the shops that closed on Saturday afternoons, the lack of friends, and the advice not to walk alone meant I was isolated and frustrated. I had no identity in this town and very little activity to occupy my long hours of unemployment. It felt like my freedom had been snatched away.

Andrew, however, was not so shocked by Port Alfred. Although it was different to Durban, where he grew up, this was Andrew's home country. He quickly adjusted. His flight training kept him busy and he fitted in happily with the welcoming community of the air school. It was exciting that he was finally learning to fly. On the days that I accompanied him, I loved to see him climb into a plane and take off, his instructor by his side.

Andrew departed early each morning to drive the ten kilometres to air school. I mostly waited in our new home, a tiny garage converted into a living area, with a stunning view over the ocean but basic facilities. Those early months were lonely. I read book after book from the local library, wondering what to do with my time. I often questioned whether we had done the right thing. Our retired neighbours were welcoming and kind when I popped over the road to visit them. Andrew and I often joked that all my Port Alfred friends were more than double my age!

Two months after our arrival, we visited a local Pentecostal church where they made an appeal for qualified teachers to work at their new Christian school. Now here was something I could do. I volunteered my services. The lady in charge looked right into my eyes and announced, 'This is from the Lord!'

She was right. I loved teaching at the brand-new El Shaddai Academy. I found purpose in the teaching and true friendship with the two other teachers. It was exciting to be involved with their initiative to provide Christian education in Port Alfred. Although I did not yet have my visa and could not earn an official salary, we never went without while we waited for my application to be approved. The Lord had opened up an unexpected opportunity for me to thrive in this land so far from home. He was asking me to trust Him and I was seeing His kindness. I was learning to trust His timing, too. If I had not been in that particular church on that particular morning, I may never have heard about this teaching position.

My spiritual trust muscles were being developed in a training gym called South Africa. I would need that muscle strength in the years to come, as God led us further and further out of our comfort zone.

Andrew and I received another major boost in trusting God a few months later. We had to make some final payments to the air school for Andrew's training. When I considered the outgoing costs, anxiety gnawed at my mind. How would we manage financially? We were stunned when God provided in an unorthodox way.

Andrew paid the bills with his UK bank card. We waited and waited for our bank balance to go down, but the money remained in our account. When Andrew checked with the air school, the clerk reassured him, 'Andrew, the bill is paid. Here is your receipt.' It was most mysterious. Andrew next contacted our bank, but there was no sign of any error in the system.

On our next UK trip, Andrew spoke to the staff at our bank, who could not give a clear answer about what had happened. Not wanting to end up with complications, Andrew paid a small bank fee so that they could carry out an investigation – but nothing untoward was found. There seemed to be no record of the transactions. 'Since you used your bank card,' they explained, 'the money could still come out of your account for up to five years afterwards.'

There was nothing more for us to do but wait and be grateful for the funds we still had. Miraculously, the money never left our account, but the air school received the sum they needed. It was inexplicable – and it was teaching us to trust that God can operate way beyond our expectations. If He was leading the way for Andrew to train as a pilot, He could provide the means. It was an exciting step forward on our journey to 'go anywhere' with our trustworthy God.

Andrew gained his commercial pilot's licence in November 2005. Early in his training, we had celebrated his very first solo flight – an exciting occasion that his fellow students had marked by throwing Andrew, fully clothed, into the 43 Air School swimming pool. Almost a year after this celebration, Andrew and I returned to England to prepare for a different kind of immersion – into the world of parenthood.

6

'For such a time as this'

Wild Lancashire winds blew icy gusts outdoors, but I was safe inside. I savoured the warmth of the hospital ward and gazed in amazement at the beautiful little miracle in my arms. Two months after Andrew and I returned to England, we were thrilled when our first child entered the world. At visiting times, I sat on my English hospital bed and smiled while Andrew held his daughter in his arms. He was bursting with pride.

Family and friends sent kind gifts when they heard about baby Esther. Happy balloons bobbed a colourful welcome and bouquets of stunning flowers cheered up the bland décor of the ward. We chose our daughter's name for two reasons. Firstly, because it means 'star' – a ray of hope and light for her generation. Secondly, because in the Bible Esther was strategic in saving her people since she was in the right place, at the right time: 'for such a time as this' (Esther 4:14). We were soon surprised to discover how appropriate her name was.

We had returned to the UK for Esther's delivery in order to be close to family. Just a couple of weeks after Esther's birth, we were sitting in the small flat we were renting in Burscough when the phone rang incessantly. I reached past my tiny daughter to answer it. My dad was on the line. 'Liz, I'm afraid we have some bad news,' he began. 'I have to go to hospital and have an operation.'

'An operation, Dad? What for?' I asked, taken aback by this unexpected news.

'The doctors have found cancer, dear. It's bowel cancer.'

I was devastated. Nevertheless, being in England for these few months meant we were just fifteen minutes down the road from my parents, on hand to help with hospital visits and with supporting my mum. I put it down to God's impeccable timing.

Six months later, Dad had recovered well enough to lead a service of thanksgiving for Esther's life at St John's Church, Burscough. We celebrated her life with friends and family – including all four of our parents.

Just a few weeks afterwards, we packed up our lovely little flat and hauled out the suitcases – again. Andrew's flying licence was only valid in South Africa, so there was no question of remaining in England. For the past six months, Andrew had taken a job as a telephone salesman for a shoe company, which paid the bills, but frustration was building. He wanted to get airborne.

We booked flights to Johannesburg at the kind invitation of a friend of Andrew's parents, John and Annabel. We had never met this lady, so her hospitality was extravagant. We were also grateful that Andrew's parents would meet us and stay with us there for a while. Having this time with them, and for them to get to know Esther more, would be special.

Our prayer was that a few weeks in Johannesburg would help us to find answers to our burning question: where would Andrew find a job to build his flying hours? Every MAF pilot needed a minimum of five hundred hours' flight experience before they could apply. How was God going to make a way for us in this next chapter of our journey?

All too soon, therefore, we were standing at the departure gate at Manchester Airport. My heart was aching. This goodbye was going to be extra hard, as we were taking my parent's first grandchild far away. Nor did we really know where we were going, or how long we would be gone. We only knew that on this pathway to 'fly planes for God in Africa', Andrew needed work in far-off South Africa.

Mum held her six-month-old granddaughter in her arms for those final moments, cooing gently to her and trying to smile. Dad held Esther's tiny hand in his until the very last minute. Then we whisked her away through security and into the departure lounge. I tried not to look back, but couldn't help it. Mum's cheeks were already tear-stained and her face was starting to crumble. I hated leaving them – they looked so forlorn. I cried all the way to Johannesburg. I heard later that Mum cried all night. Parting is always unavoidably painful.

We stepped off the plane into the sunshine of South Africa and were met by another set of grandparents, their faces wreathed in smiles, excitement high as they reached out welcoming arms for their granddaughter. As I looked across at Esther, I was reminded of the meaning behind her name: 'for such a time as this'. This was a new chapter. God had just shown us how He works out the timing of events to perfection. Now it was time to trust Him for the next step.

7

Inopportunely stopped by police

Johannesburg was a dry, sun-filled, hectic city. It welcomed us for two months, allowing Andrew to pass his ATPL aviation exams and giving him time to job hunt. One day, while Esther and I were sitting by the swimming pool of our gracious hostess, Andrew burst out of the glass conservatory doors and into the dappled, shady garden. 'Liz, there's a vacancy in Port Alfred for a flight instructor!' he called.

I jumped up. 'That's great!' I said – and we smiled at this excellent news.

A few days later, we drove the two-day journey down to South Africa's Eastern Cape and back to Port Alfred. We moved straight into a small, furnished cottage a ten-minute walk from Port Alfred's beautiful, windswept beach. Andrew passed his instructor's rating exams and signed a two-year contract with 43 Air School, which would give him more than one thousand hours of flying experience. God had faithfully provided the answers to our questions – again. We even had a time frame: two years in Port Alfred, and then Andrew could apply for MAF. It seemed almost unreal.

Of course, those two years were not without moments of drama. On Sunday 9 December 2007, Andrew and I set off to drive to Port Elizabeth Hospital, a two-hour drive from our home. I was expecting our new baby – and he was definitely on his way. While Esther remained back at the cottage with Andrew's parents, who were visiting for a few weeks, our car zipped along the main road – past the seaside town of Kenton-on-Sea and towards the city of Port Elizabeth.

Suddenly, we encountered a checkpoint set up by police halfway between Port Alfred and the city of Port Elizabeth. An energetic policeman flagged Andrew down and demanded that we stop our car immediately. I squirmed in discomfort. 'Andrew, tell him we can't stop,' I pleaded. Sweat began to form on my forehead and my anxiety level rose sharply.

My swollen stomach contracted as Andrew wound down the window of our car. He then leaned out to negotiate with the burly South African policeman blocking the road. 'Papers and licence,' he began...

The policeman was cut short, though, when Andrew frantically gestured towards me and interrupted with,

'Sir, my wife is in labour and about to have a baby! Please, we need to get to the hospital. Can you let us through?'

It probably seemed like the classic excuse, but if a shadow of doubt crossed that policeman's face, it was erased as soon as he bent to look inside our car. He witnessed for himself my heaving stomach and anxious face. 'Let them through – she's having a baby!' he yelled, as he hurriedly indicated for the checkpoint barriers to be lifted. We were given a special concession and drove by all the policemen, who hastily removed all obstacles in our way.

We arrived at Port Elizabeth Hospital just in time for Ben to be welcomed into the world. South African midwife Rosie was stunned by his speedy arrival. I was simply thankful that we made it in time, despite the police checkpoint! Andrew and I were thrilled to meet our son – what a handsome, well-timed gift. To this day, our son Ben is rightly proud of his claim to Africa, and delighted that he was the only one of his siblings to be born on the African continent. He loves this solidarity with his South African father.

Ben was a delightfully cuddly baby and had the startling ability, like many infants, of making his presence heard – as my dad was to discover. My parents travelled to South Africa to meet their first grandson when Ben was three months old. It was Dad's first visit to the African continent. He loved the sunshine and Port Alfred's coastal charms. Taking Ben for a stroll one day, Dad set off happily, his new grandson strapped securely in the pram. I heard, rather than saw, my father and my son returning home. Their return was heralded by the barking of the neighbourhood dogs and the shouting of my baby, demonstrating his excellent lung capacity. Dad shot through our wooden garden gates, out of breath and wearing a shocked expression.

'Oh, Elizabeth,' he said, puffing. 'Ben hasn't stopped screaming for our entire walk! Every time we passed a house, all the dogs joined in – the whole street is full of noise! I was so embarrassed, I raced home as fast as I could!'

Six months after Ben was born, we started to connect with MAF. With more than one thousand hours and two years of flying experience, Andrew finally had the entry requirements needed to apply as a mission pilot. Skype meetings followed, then we filled in the relevant application forms. As MAF is a mission organisation, and since the family accompanies the job holder on placements, our application was for me as well as Andrew. I enjoyed filling in the forms – so much of our recent cross-cultural life in England and South Africa seemed relevant to the questions.

We were ecstatic when MAF emailed back and invited us for an interview in England. We decided to pack up our life in South Africa and take our young family back to the UK for the interview. It had taken more than four years to get to this point – surely God would not steer us in a different direction now?

8

A rollercoaster ride

The grey, cloudy skies and the chill of the wintry winds were a shock to our system as we arrived back in England's winter from South Africa's summer. Our return in January 2009 had been marked with drama as our planned overnight journey ended up as a three-day haul. We had so many delays that we even missed our 'welcome back' party! Finally, our bedraggled, exhausted family of four made it to my parent's home. We were laden with car seats, suitcases and bags overflowing with nappies and toys for three-year-old Esther and one-year-old Ben. My parent's home was invaded. Their sedate rhythm of retirement moved out as their grandchildren moved in.

Andrew and I travelled down to Kent with Esther, Ben and my parents, ready to begin the interview process for MAF. This was a critical point in our journey. After all the changes and moves between South Africa and England, we hoped we had heard correctly that the Lord really was calling Andrew to 'fly planes for God in Africa'.

Imagine our confusion when the interview process did not go well. We stepped out of the interviews uncertain. Despite our efforts – moving to South Africa and leaving behind the securities of London, despite the miraculous provision we had seen for Andrew's pilot training, and despite the evidence of God leading us over four years, had we really misunderstood the direction we had followed? There was no overwhelming clarity, but rather a sense of disappointment as we came away from the MAF offices feeling that they were not able to give us the positive answer we hoped for.

A kind of darkness, a heaviness of spirit, descended. As Andrew's wife, I felt particularly bad for him. I had never seen him so down and unsure. It is times like these, however, when our kind Father God sends in the reinforcements. He had blessed us with many wonderful friends. Their words of encouragement, their phone calls and their prayers gave us strength to look up and keep our eyes on God, even when we were starting to ask, 'If MAF say no, what shall we do next?' They reminded us that, whatever the outcome, none of the past four years would be wasted – because God is not a God of waste.

We were relieved a few days later when one of the MAF interview panel called Andrew and invited him for further interviews. Our prayer warriors lined up and prayed with us that, whatever the decision might be, it would be the right one for Andrew and the right one for MAF. They prayed for peace and a clear mind for Andrew.

After this second round of interviews, Andrew travelled back to my parent's home. He had only been home a short while when his mobile started to ring. Answering the call, Andrew heard MAF's human resources manager inform him, 'We're delighted to accept you and your family as part of MAF.' We could barely believe it. Great whoops of joy and happy celebrations followed.

From a low dip to a high, this was a rollercoaster ride. Looking back on that time, it was an important lesson. Maybe the years in South Africa, the pilot training and Andrew's years as a flight instructor had made us overconfident in our own investment. Maybe God wanted to get our attention back to Him and our focus back on prayer? If His calling was for Andrew to be a MAF pilot, then it had to be *God* who opened the door, not a series of easy interviews and quick answers.

This experience also highlighted for me how much we need the support of God's people. When we were uncertain, they rallied around and encouraged us with kindness and prayer. When we told them that Andrew had been accepted as a missionary pilot, they celebrated with us. Their solidarity was such a gift.

A few weeks later, we excitedly signed a job contract with MAF. They explained to us how important it is to have a network of supporters to pray for and encourage us, to give to MAF for our financial support and to be part of the venture – but we already knew this fact. Over the past four years, we had experienced the love and support of so many people. To this day, we remain indebted to each person who has joined for some or all of our MAF journey. These faithful, prayerful, caring people are as much a part of the work as those who go overseas.

In February, we moved into a small terraced house in Burscough while we worked to raise funds for our placement overseas. We joined in several training courses and Andrew underwent five weeks of intense flying training in America. One afternoon, shortly after Andrew's return from the USA, I was busy cooking dinner for the family when the shrill ring of our landline telephone cut into my domestic task. I answered quickly and then stood with an enthusiastic smile on my face as I heard a voice from the MAF office say, 'Your first placement will be Dodoma, Tanzania.'

After I hung up, I couldn't wait to share the news. 'Andrew,' I called out, 'we're going to Tanzania!'

In November, we packed up our temporary Lancashire home, shoved everything into a shipping container and took our two children and our suitcases to Manchester Airport. As ever, the goodbyes were hard – but this time there was certainty. My pilot husband led the way as we boarded an international flight and headed to Tanzania for his new role.

We were on our way to East Africa!

Part Three

Tanzania

NOVEMBER 2009 – JANUARY 2014

9

A learning ground

It all started on 10 November 2009. Our overnight flight from England set us down early that morning in a sticky and humid Dar es Salaam. It felt incredible to finally be in Tanzania as a family – on our first-ever MAF placement. One of the Dar-based MAF pilots came to meet us and to fly us onwards to Dodoma. He led us across the busy apron of the airport to the waiting MAF plane, his blue uniform dotted with perspiration as he loaded our hefty suitcases into the pod of the small aeroplane. Just a short while later, he expertly took off from the searing heat of Dar es Salaam's runway.

How incredible to see Tanzania laid out below, the tropical coastline gradually giving way to vast, open dryness. We were glued to our windows, admiring the views of our new host country. Three-year-old Esther, filled with wonder, leaned over to look down, while one-year-old Ben sat dazed by the experience.

We landed less than two hours later in Dodoma, the less developed location that was to be our home for the next four years. Although officially the capital city of Tanzania, Dodoma was more like a small town. Very few streets in Dodoma had tarmac surfaces, many buildings were single storey and the 'city' could not boast a single traffic light. Lazy cows wandered the side streets between the town centre and the MAF compound which would be our new home.

Flat, dry, hot and dusty: this was Dodoma. Friendly, warm and welcoming: this was our MAF team. As a group, they hurried down to meet us at the tiny airport located right next to the MAF housing. With happy smiles, we were ushered into a generous, single-storey home whose cool concrete floors and shady overhangs provided welcome relief from the beating sun. Esther and Ben were shown into their bedroom. Kind neighbours had covered their bedroom door with pictures of aeroplanes, flowers and animals, drawn by the other MAF children – their new playmates.

Andrew and I were made to feel at home as we were led into our kitchen. The fridge and the larder shelves had been filled with food. The cupboard above the kettle contained something wonderful – tea bags! All we needed to do was make that welcome cup of tea, sit down and refresh ourselves. Both Esther and Ben quickly discovered that outside our front door, the sandy, dusty compound was a fun and sociable play area.

Immediately behind our new home loomed the MAF hangar. Its enormous white bulk, filled with planes, engineers and staff, was a bustling hub of action in the week and a silent witness to the work of MAF in the evenings and weekends. It was an adjustment to be living next to the centre of avionics repairs and engine testing. The noise of planes taking off and landing on the other side of the hangar could also be overwhelming since we had windows that could not be fully closed. On the other hand, the staff in the hangar office could hear everything happening in the back end of our house. They had to adjust to the busy noise of a young family, with all the yells, laughter and crying that small children bring. Our daily lives were suddenly more public.

We spent four remarkable years on Tanzanian soil. This was the country where our children gained their early impressions of life, where Esther and Ben first attended primary school and where our third-born took his first steps.

It was a land of sunshine and where the poignant Swahili words of the national anthem never failed to stir me, declaring God's blessings over Africa and blessings, unity and peace over the people of Tanzania. On Friday mornings, I stood with other parents at the school assembly, moved to tears by the patriotic singing that threatened to burst the concrete walls of the school hall – so loud and enthusiastic were the voices that belted out this prayer for Africa, for Tanzania.

There was so much I loved about Tanzania. The warm welcome of strangers and the hospitality of our Tanzanian friends. The generosity of people who had little but knew how to share. The energetic, rhythmic dancing and singing in the local churches and school. The sparkling sunshine of Dodoma's early mornings before heat fried the land. The accepting smiles of our Tanzanian colleagues and neighbours. The vivid colours worn by the ladies in town and of the flowers on our compound. The rich scent of rain as it moved across the land, bringing welcome relief at the end of Dodoma's harsh dry season.

When we drove to the coastal city of Dar es Salaam, I appreciated the gentle beauty of the Morogoro hills we passed, before then feasting my eyes on Tanzania's coastal views – the lively blue of the Indian Ocean and the pristine, sandy beaches. In the west of the country, I loved the brilliant green of the tea fields. In the north, I marvelled at the majestic Mount Kilimanjaro. Tanzania is a land of stunning contrasts.

I discovered that Tanzania is a country with a culture unlike any I had previously known. I wrestled, though, with the embarrassment of being different in a foreign land, of being pointed at as people shouted, *'mzungu!'* (white person). There were other aspects I found difficult. The long, dry season was unbearably hot, where every day felt the same, the weather never changing and the sun stinging our skin. I missed the marking of different seasons too – even Christmas was barely acknowledged in Dodoma. For me, this created a tiring monotony.

Dodoma was so far inland and its climate so dry that I was surprised to find myself missing the blue of water and the greenery of England. We would go for walks and picnics around the Dodoma dam, but at the height of the dry season, we found only sun-baked, cracked mud in the basin and all the trees were the same dull brown – until the rains flooded Dodoma with life.

Tanzania was the country where I learnt to deal with scorpions (scream loudly and run for help), rodents (scream even louder, run even faster) and snakes (stifle the scream, back away, then run!). Demands for our money and help were incessant. Poverty was an everyday reality, so I learnt to pray for wisdom as we tried to decipher the best ways to help.

Although I struggled to adapt, Tanzania worked its way deep into my heart. When we left four years later, I found it difficult to pull free from the roots we put down in this sun-drenched land. It was also the place where we learnt what it meant to be part of Mission Aviation Fellowship. It was eye-opening to witness the positive difference that MAF flights could make to peoples' lives. I discovered that deep friendships formed quickly among our team, where life was lived in a tight-knit community that shared a common faith and common goal.

It was exciting, rewarding, enlivening, frustrating and exhausting all at the same time. It was an adventure and a privilege – and a training ground for many more years with MAF, across three more countries.

10

Flying planes for God

After our arrival in Tanzania, Andrew and I initially spent time away at language school to master the basics of Swahili. However, once we returned to Dodoma and settled in, Andrew became busy with his pilot responsibilities. It was amazing to see my husband, smart in his uniform, a MAF pilot at last!

It took me a while to get used to the idea that I could take our children for a short stroll and end up in the MAF hangar. Just a few extra steps took us on to the airstrip of Dodoma's small airport, where we could witness Andrew taking off or landing a MAF plane. I never imagined a place like this when Andrew first talked about 'flying planes for God in Africa'.

Stories of how MAF flights were being used by God to touch lives in Tanzania inspired me and encouraged Andrew. He flew a Cessna 206, a small plane with just six seats which could land easily on the remote strips of the Tanzanian bush. Deliberately keeping his camera in his bag, Andrew often returned home from flights with photos. I gazed at these, taking in the scenes which brought Andrew's work colourfully to life: medical teams hard at work in isolated villages; doctors administering vaccines or checking the weight of tiny babies, hung securely in a faded cloth, suspended from weighing scales attached to the branches of an acacia tree; anxious mothers leaning in watchfully, their faces sometimes etched with tribal markings and the bright colours of their clothes diminished by the dust.

In another photo, doctors were checking the health of pregnant mothers. They used a rickety mud hut as a temporary bush clinic. Without the aeroplane flying in these medical teams, the mothers would have to walk for hours, or even days, to access pre-natal care – or to obtain vaccines for their young children.

Other photographs transported me into the heart of a Tanzanian village. Hordes of children were huddled together around a team of evangelists, some taking shelter from the merciless sun in the shade created by the wings of the MAF plane. Sat on the baked earth, the children's faces were turned towards the enthusiastic evangelists, who shared exciting stories of the Jesus who loves them. The evangelists broadcast their message further by rigging up a small microphone to a mobile-phone speaker. In the background I could therefore see a group of tall herdsmen, leaning on wooden staffs as they listened to the life-giving talks. Goats and occasional cows completed the scene.

Another image was of Elisha, a Masai evangelist, his dark eyes deep with understanding and peace. Andrew told me of Elisha's deep love for Jesus and for his people. He used MAF planes to visit the small villages of his region, keen to tell his people more of the Jesus who brings hope. While visiting all the villages on foot in this mountainous, inhospitable terrain would take days, the MAF plane made it possible in hours.

Yet another photograph was of Andrew standing next to the plane with Elisha and a younger Tanzanian man. 'This is Abraham,' Andrew said. 'He was one of the most powerful witch doctors in the area.' Abraham's life used to be steeped in the shady deeds of fear and darkness. His powerful position kept his community locked in fear. Yet here Abraham's eyes were alight with a new power: one which comes from love and our Father of heavenly light. Elisha and the Masai evangelists he worked with were able to bring news of life-giving freedom to men like Abraham. We considered it a huge privilege to hear these testimonies and to be a small part of their stories through MAF.

Over the four years we were in Tanzania, I looked on while my husband and the other MAF pilots transported medical teams into difficult locations. Doctors, nurses and medical specialists like opticians and dentists all flew with MAF, bringing help and transformation to patients who may never be able to access these services otherwise. MAF carried out medical evacuations in critical situations.

They supported remote hospitals by delivering essential supplies. They carried building materials and water pumps to places where road journeys would either be impossible, or take days.

On two occasions, the children and I joined Andrew on a flight to Magumbua, a small village in the bush. We visited the clinic where American doctor John Eager worked and then spent the day with his wonderful family at their home – while Andrew flew a medical team from their clinic to Birise, another remote village. I was inspired by the Eager family's hard work in this rural community so cut off from modern amenities.

MAF planes are sometimes referred to as 'the Samaritan's donkey'. MAF is not a missionary organisation in the conventional sense of the phrase, but their planes allow 'Good Samaritans' to get where they need to be to do good works, especially when those places are hard to reach by land transport. It was always a delight to meet some of these Good Samaritans, hear their real stories and see photographs that showed how MAF helped.

In South Africa, I had wrestled that giant of Doubt, sometimes questioning: *Did God really call my husband to fly planes for His work? Was it worth quitting London to move to this unknown place?* Now I was able to witness for myself the life-changing work of MAF as they carried out their vision: to see 'isolated people physically and spiritually transformed in Christ's name'. Without a doubt, every single step we had taken was worthwhile.

It had taken four years and more money than we had to complete Andrew's pilot training, but God never failed us. He had promised to lead us forward – and had done exactly that. He is ever faithful. Always.

11

The ups and downs of community life

Community was an essential part of our four Dodoma years. I did mostly love this collective life – but sometimes found it claustrophobic. The Western mindset encourages independence and self-sufficiency. Now I had to adjust to living where our neighbours knew our every move!

Designed as a kind of rectangle, our compound houses were located close to one another. The windows were slatted, louvre, glass panels which never fully closed. Fly netting provided protection from mosquitoes, but was not so great at preventing noise from coming in or going out. We learnt to tailor the volume of our phone calls back to the UK so that the whole community didn't have to overhear. I envied the neighbours who spoke unfamiliar languages because they could have privacy. Our conversations in English could nearly always be understood by others.

In the centre of our compound was a sparkling swimming pool. It was like a central hub. I have to admit, it felt incongruous to see colleagues in swimming gear just half an hour after observing them at work in their MAF uniforms. However, the blissful coolness of the water was such a welcome relief from the blistering African sun that these thoughts evaporated as quickly as the puddles around the pool. Many were the birthday parties and celebrations that we enjoyed clustered around that refreshing oasis.

At night, when our young children screamed, I cringed, knowing that our neighbours could hear their yells. When other people's babies screamed, I sighed with relief and rolled over in my bed. It was good to know that right then I was not the one who needed to get up and that our family wasn't the only one with noisy children.

The children loved compound life. Their friends lived right on their doorstep. Since the compound was secured with guarded, locked gates, they had freedom to explore. When we were home, we left the wooden front door open to allow a breeze. The simple fly screens pulled across the entrance to each house were light enough for small children to open. I might come through to the lounge and find several extra children playing with mine on the cool, concrete floor. It was a happy scene.

Sometimes, though, life in close quarters was stressful.

'Mum! MUM!' shouted Esther. I heard my daughter calling, looked through the kitchen window and saw Esther fighting over her bike with another small child.

'Oh, really!' I sighed to myself, before responding, 'Wait a minute, Esther, I'm coming.' Annoyed at having to resolve their argument, I pushed open the fly-screen door and stepped into our sparse, dry garden, telling both children off sharply – and upsetting them in the process. The other child went running across the compound back to her house, crying and unhappy – and now I had also upset her mother! Her mum's response was grace-filled, though – and taught me early on that a small compound has very little space for resentment. Our friendship was in fact strengthened by this neighbour's truthful, kind handling of my outburst. In a multi-cultural community, where each family has different approaches to family life, it was an ongoing challenge to accept one another's differences and to respond with love. That was simply a reality of living so close together, whether on this or future MAF compounds. I often made mistakes, needing forgiveness or to forgive.

Being part of a community meant sharing our lives. Living in a distant land, neighbours and friends became like extended family. Kind packages were dropped off at the door when we were sick, and meal invitations were issued when Andrew was away and I was alone with small children. Medical help was given when our children were ill. Small parcels were lovingly wrapped for Esther, Ben and Joel at birthdays. That was a bonus because mail was slow to arrive; one parcel for Ben arrived ten months after it had been posted in England!

Our community also offered practical support in times of drama, like the day our Toyota Prado decided to break down. It was a typical warm afternoon as I set off to drive the children to a hotel swimming pool. We bumped noisily down a muddy side street, veering around potholes, when suddenly the car lurched violently forward, the engine roared and then our car shuddered to a rebellious halt. Confused, I tried pressing the accelerator, thinking that perhaps I had driven into a pothole, but all that happened was an unusual grating sound and angrier roaring.

'Children, stay in your seats!' I ordered, glancing back at my little ones as I swung open the door and jumped down to the muddy road. I was shocked by what I saw. There was no pothole under my vehicle. Instead, the front-left wheel had somehow worked itself out of place and was now jammed at an angle under the body of the car. We were stranded on a quiet side street, although by now a crowd of curious onlookers were gathering and starting to offer advice. I took out my phone to call the mechanic, but realised that I had not saved his number. There was no point calling Andrew. Like many of the times I had a crisis in Tanzania, he was away overnight for MAF flights.

Thankfully, though, I had the number of our MAF friend Patricia. I knew she'd be good in a crisis. She soon appeared, followed closely by the mechanic she had called. He quickly assessed the damage and arranged for a tow truck. Apparently, an essential bearing had worn away, causing the entire wheel and steering mechanism to collapse. Patricia, putting her own plans on hold, kindly delivered us safely to the MAF compound. I was grateful to Patricia for her help and to God for our safety, since a fault like this could have caused a serious accident if I had been driving at speed.

On another occasion, it was our French neighbour and MAF engineer Pierre who stepped in on hearing my shouts for assistance. I was in the kitchen when I sensed a black creature scurrying across the floor. Glancing down, I froze in fear at the sight of the large scorpion advancing towards us, its tail raised threateningly. I scooped up my baby and run outdoors, yelling for help. Pierre was there in a flash, brandishing the dustpan I gratefully handed him on his way past. A few moments later, the scorpion was successfully captured in the dustpan and our home was safe enough for my young children again.

Our compound came alive during boisterous birthday parties when kids ran wild and enjoyed crazy games. It was an advantage living next to the airfield. For example, I was delighted when the Tanzanian firefighters based at the airfield graciously agreed to drive their fire engine across to the hangar for Ben's fifth birthday party. Ben and his guests were invited aboard and allowed to use the water hose. For his aviation-themed sixth birthday party, Ben and his friends walked across to the MAF hangar and each child took turns to climb into the cockpit of a Cessna 206 aeroplane and pose for a photograph which they took home afterwards. These were unique birthday opportunities.

At Christmas, although we missed our home cultures and far-off families, we celebrated with our Dodoma friends. I was thankful for these friends God gave us, both within and without our team. We often had to let friends go as they moved on elsewhere or returned to their home countries. Each time, we cried sad tears and missed those people who had become like family. Then new friends came and the process of forming deep bonds started all over again. Our community was constantly changing; we had to learn to adapt.

12

Lost in translation

Her *kanga* garment wrapped tightly around her waist, her brightly coloured T-shirt complementing the oranges and yellows of her African garb, Mama Kambenga hurried up to our door. *'Hodi, hodi!'*

I heard the call of her deep, rich African voice and came through to the living room, where I could see my Tanzanian friend – an enthusiastic evangelist – smiling through the fly-screen netting of our door. *'Karibu!'* I answered her with the Swahili welcome, inviting her into our home.

Mama Kambenga slipped off her loose sandals and stepped up to the floor of our lounge. I was pleased to see her. Her warm smile reflected the heat of this land. Her energetic entrance displayed the vibrancy of her personality, so willing to help me deepen my understanding of her country, Tanzanian culture and its

Swahili language. Every Tuesday morning, she opened the door of my mind a little further to embrace the richness of this African nation.

The beautiful colours worn not just by Mama Kambenga but by other Tanzanian friends were in stark contrast to the brown, dust-covered hues that covered most of semi-arid Dodoma. Dust was a fact of life. We could polish the furniture in the morning and then use our fingers to write our names in a fine, brown powder by the end of the afternoon.

Many Dodoma residents did not know English, so my weekly meetings with Mama Kambenga were a lifeline. I needed Swahili to go shopping, to visit the doctor and to converse with my dedicated, hard-working Tanzanian house help. Because Swahili was such an essential skill in Dodoma, language learning had started long before my appointments with Mama Kambenga. I met her several months after we arrived in Tanzania and she built on the basics I had already acquired.

Our family's Swahili lessons began just two weeks after our arrival in Tanzania. We went together to a language learning camp in Iringa, a nine-hour drive south-west of Dodoma. When I say camp, I mean camp! The language school was situated deep in a beautiful, rural campsite, where lush, grassy banks lined the fast-flowing Ruaha River. Guests were housed in tents, *bandas* (thatched huts) or wooden huts. When we arrived, we were directed to our accommodation: a round, stone *banda*. From the outside, it had a rustic appeal. Inside, it was cool and basic.

There was a small bathroom on one side, with a shower head that sprinkled us with water pumped from the river. Even if we scrubbed hard with soap, we never managed to lose the whiff of stale river water and our skin bore a slight river-coloured tinge for the two months we stayed there.

Language school was a sort of initiation. Day after day, our heads buzzed with conjugating Swahili verbs and piecing together a language which works like a jigsaw puzzle. I enjoyed the humour and dedication of our teachers. I loved learning a new language, but I didn't enjoy the disruption our children felt.

Esther and Ben were cared for by a young Tanzanian teenager. Culturally, a babysitter rarely plays with her charges, so Emma simply watched Esther and Ben. Every morning, she walked them down to play by the riverbank and ensured they were safe, but she didn't engage them in activities. Besides, she had very little English. Sometimes, the sound of Ben crying drifted on the breeze from the riverbank and reached our classroom. For comfort, Ben sucked his thumbs so hard that the skin on them blistered. It hurt to see him so unhappy. I resorted to bribing him with tubes of chocolate to get him to stay with Emma while we studied. He would then waddle off, his chubby legs getting browner by the day. In his hot little hand he would clutch his melting treats, but he was often on the brink of tears.

Night after night, we battled with a screaming Ben. He didn't sleep well and frequently had an upset stomach, filling nappy after nappy with foul-smelling, bright yellow liquid. We went through tubs of cream to soothe the angry rash around his nappy area. His little body struggled to adapt to new food and a different standard of hygiene.

Esther, meanwhile, had spectacular, vivid nightmares for the first two weeks of language school, screaming into the night. 'There's a bear! A lion!' she would shriek.

At breakfast one morning, we discussed her nightmares with other students who had overhead her night-time shouts. 'Is she on anti-malaria medication?' they asked.

'Yes, we're giving her Larium,' we replied. These more seasoned missionaries shook their heads knowingly. 'Larium can cause horrible hallucinations, even for children,' they told us. On their recommendation, we made the switch from Larium to Malarone – and what a happy transformation that brought! From then on, Esther slept peacefully and the frightening side-effects of Larium-induced hallucinations left her.

Ben celebrated his second birthday at language school. Five weeks later, Esther celebrated her fourth birthday at the campsite. The staff loved celebrations and made the birthdays fun for the children. We were amused at the 'birthday crown' the staff placed on their heads, made of an old Blue-Band margarine tub, cut at the top into a jagged crown shape and spray-painted gold. Ben and then Esther reigned supreme over enormous, colourful birthday cakes, large enough to feed the many people staying at the campsite. After dinner, everyone joined in with singing

'Happy Birthday!' The singing was cheerful, lighting up the atmosphere with joy that was *almost* as bright as the luminous icing on the cakes.

Language school was an incredible learning experience, culturally as well as linguistically. It did not, however, prevent me from making some terrible bloopers in Swahili during our four years in Tanzania. I once asked my house lady for help to clean up the 'sin' in our fridge. Jane looked at me in confusion, her dark eyebrows raised. As she stood silently and unmoving by the kitchen sink, my mistake suddenly dawned on me. I had muddled up the word 'sin' (*dhambi*) with 'blood' (*damu*). Fortunately, Jane had a good sense of humour and laughed when I explained that a bag of beef had spilt blood all over the bottom shelf of our fridge.

Jane also boosted my language skills, since we always spoke Swahili together while working together around our family home. She shocked me with tales of how her husband mistreated her before he left home to take another wife – and how he ended up poisoned by his second wife. I heard chilling tales of terrible conditions from Jane's stay in the local hospital.

Still, my Swahili was always at domestic level, so my continuing lessons with good friend Mama Kambenga were vital – living in a different culture is always a learning curve; every experience is part of the journey.

13

Facing my fears

I stepped gingerly over the mud and the rotten, wooden board haphazardly slung over the murky waters of a drain. I caught my balance on the dirt pathway which ran narrowly between the wooden market stalls. The dirty tarpaulin overhead flapped and dipped with the light breeze, releasing glimpses of sunlight into this dingy world.

The metallic smell of unrefrigerated meat mixed with the odour of putrid drains. Sweaty bodies jostled one another, and the shouts of vendors mixed with the cries of children's voices. All this created the chaos of Dodoma's market. Further on, tables loaded with bright green fruit offered an appealing freshness. Mounds of green mangoes, green oranges and green lemons were piled high on the rickety table. I drew closer, then stopped to examine them.

'*Habari za leo?*' ('How is the day?') I greeted the stallkeeper, sorely conscious of my pale, foreign skin in this African setting, but determined to use my newly acquired language skills.

'*Nzuri, dada,*' ('Good, my sister') came the reply. I loved it when the return greeting included me as 'sister'. Any differences between us diminished a little.

We discussed the price of fruit. A young lad in rumpled T-shirt and jeans took my basket and loaded it with mangoes, oranges and a handful of hard lemons. I was still getting used to all the fruit being green in Dodoma. Each fruit was recognisable by its size and texture rather than its colour. Rummaging in the small bag tightly slung across my chest, I pulled out some dog-eared bank notes, faded and smelling of stale perspiration. Handing them over, I was instructed to wait for my change. Although nervous about random pickpockets as I navigated through the market stalls, I had no doubts the scrupulously honest stallkeepers would always hand me back the correct change, or even extra if they did not have the exact coins needed.

I stood to one side, dodging the hurried porters who bombarded their way through the tight spaces between stalls, their backs doubled over with heavy sacks of charcoal, flour and sugar. They whistled a warning to move us out of their way, the weight of their loads making it hard for them to slow down. Having almost been knocked sideways by these loads more than once, I quickly learnt to step aside.

With my change now returned, I turned to the stall a little way down the passage to bargain over the price of a kilogram of wheat grain. I would be milling this into brown flour later, to add texture to our home-made bread. Next, moving carefully through the dim labyrinth, I made my way towards the entrance to purchase the heavier potatoes and carrots. I would choose the vendor carefully. Yet one day just like this, I received a nasty shock at the carrot stall.

That morning, I had jumped out of the school minibus eager to get my market shop over as quickly as possible (not an easy ask). Now, I suddenly stood stock-still. I had watched horrified as the vendor plunged his hands into the mountain of carrots – and pulled out dead rat after dead rat, flinging them to the ground as each dead rodent was unearthed. Gripped with a strange fascination, I stared at the ever-growing pile of stiff rats.

'Ha! Mzungu! Usiogope!' ('White lady! Don't be afraid!') The vendor gave me a wry grin, having gently mocked me. Feeling awkwardly out of place in my fear, I gave a half wave to the vendor and turned away.

My appetite for carrots had seriously waned, but I told myself firmly that this is why we wash all our fresh produce with Milton, the baby-sterilising solution. Plus, carrots are peeled, so surely any traces of rat would then be gone? I determined to go and buy carrots at a stall which had a smaller pile of vegetables – maybe that would mean fewer rats had been partying in the mass of fresh produce?

I have always had a great revulsion for rodents. One Iringa night, when our family was attending our initial language camp, I lay rigid on the sagging mattress in the stone *banda*, listening for the scratch of dreaded rats. At dinner that evening, a campsite guest had related dreadful tales of waking at night to find rats sitting on their bed and running over their baby's cot! Such stories made my skin crawl. I grabbed my torch and flashed it around the eaves. Phew! There were no rats – just lizards chasing mosquitoes for a night-time snack. When, a week later, we moved into a wooden hut further up the hill, I was grateful to escape our *banda* which was apparently notorious for rodent visitors.

The kitchen staff at Iringa once filled a cage with scraggly-looking rodents they had caught scampering close to the food cupboards. Ben was fascinated, but I could not bring myself to look in the cage. Knowing so many rats had been in the kitchen was enough to distract me from my Swahili verbs the rest of that day.

It was not just rats who ran wild along the grassy riverbank. One afternoon, I had my first encounter with a dangerous Tanzanian reptile. I was taking Esther and Ben for a stroll before I started my Swahili homework. My children followed me down a narrow path, where the grass either side drooped down in ragged, green tendrils taller than my children. I heard something rustle on the path in front of me. Hackles stood up on my neck – and suddenly, I saw it! A long, grey snake, slithering just a few feet in front of my little ones. My instinct was to scream, but I knew that screaming could cause the snake to strike, so I backed up and gently pushed Esther, then her brother, down the path in the other direction.

'There's a snake,' I whispered to Esther. Alarmed, she looked up at me, her blue eyes wide, then turned and moved as fast as her short legs could carry her. I scooped up Ben and hurried after Esther. As soon as we were at a safe distance, I yelled, 'Snake!'

This is one English word which is universally recognised. The Tanzanian workers reacted quickly. Later, they showed us the headless body of a cobra – a dangerous species. That afternoon, I learnt the Swahili word for snake: *nyoka* – a word I will never forgot.

Occasionally, one of my children joined me at the hectic market in Dodoma. Their presence always meant extra smiles from the vendors, who loved to meet the children and welcomed them kindly. Conversations around Ben were interesting, as I told them that this was my white African boy, born on their continent. Grinning widely, market-sellers reached for Ben's hand. They pumped it enthusiastically, sometimes simultaneously stroking his blond hair. Occasionally, they asked where we came from. If I replied, 'Liverpool,' they asked if I knew the LFC footballers. This was a great chance to prolong conversations and gain new vocabulary.

My white skin and floundering Swahili made me stand out when market shopping in Dodoma. Venturing out of my comfort zone made me nervous, but I was learning to overcome my fear of humiliation. Coupled with my anxiety was a sense of jubilant triumph each time I returned home, my baskets brimming with healthy food. I came away pleased with the language practice and smiling from the banter with the stall-holders.

14

Feeling the heat in the kitchen

Back in the kitchen with my fresh produce, a different battle was underway between my rational self and my emotional self. Sadly, my emotions were far more exercised than my reasoning. Rational Liz was telling me not to mind when the domestic chores went wrong, but Emotional Liz wanted to scream and cry when facing the culinary challenges of those early Dodoma days. In the UK, and even in South Africa, my meals used many ready-made ingredients. That kind of cooking already seemed a million miles away.

Yet another of my cakes had flopped. It sat sadly on the wooden work surface, next to a rather sour-smelling, curdled tub of home-made yoghurt. I stared at these disasters and fought the urge to cry. Again. I was battling an overwhelming sense of inadequacy. How could I adequately feed my young family in this slowly developing city, where each meal had to be made from scratch? I tried not to compare myself with the other MAF wives who seemed oh-so competent in the kitchen. Was I a failing missionary pilot's wife?

We were twelve households over two compounds in Dodoma. The other families welcomed us with warmth and kindness, frequently inviting us for meals. Every one prepared for us was delicious – and I sat in secret awe, wondering how on earth I could ever make meals like this for guests, or even for my family.

Being part of a multi-national MAF team was a multi-cultural cuisine experience. Neighbours popped over with Irish sourdough bread, Swiss salads or Swedish meatballs. Dutch, New Zealander, Australian and American neighbours brought over jams, cakes and biscuits. I was thankful for each gift – but felt so inexperienced. I had never baked bread, or made jam or yoghurt – and never had it crossed my mind that I could make pastry.

Each week, we were emailed a rota, listing when and who we would be hosting. We were simply expected to provide hospitality for staff visiting from other countries or cities. While Andrew flew his planes up to dizzy heights and brought hope to those in isolated communities, I was teetering on a steep ladder of learning and uselessness.

The frequent tears of frustration on my face felt almost as hot as the flames in my Tanzanian gas cooker.

The East African heat, pouring through my kitchen windows, enhanced my exasperation. I had less patience to battle the cockroaches in my dark, wooden cupboard and the weevils in my flour, and was irritable with my long-suffering husband. This was where I had to call out to Jesus for patience, for more grace – and for my bread to please rise!

I was learning, though, that where the Lord calls, He equips. One of my saving graces was a short, serious-looking, older Tanzanian lady. Slightly stooped through years of sheer hard work, her dark skin wrinkled and her walk slow and deliberate, this was Jane Manda – my first house helper, whom I have already mentioned. Initially, I had been adamant that I would not need house help. I did not want to make someone else work in my home. How naïve I was! I was taken to one side by one of my British neighbours, who gently explained to me that providing employment for this lady meant provision for her and her entire extended family. *Not* to employ someone in my home would be seen as an arrogant gesture – a refusal to share my perceived Western wealth with the local community.

I soon realised that having Jane to help us was one of the greatest blessings of our home life. What would I have done without her? Jane helped to keep the prolific dust at bay. She meticulously ironed our clothes to kill mango flies, which lay eggs in fresh laundry and later hatch into your skin. An expert cook, she knew a host of recipes and was keenly aware of the kinds of food a westerner like me might enjoy. Having worked for more than twenty years with foreigners based in Dodoma, she carefully modelled the basics of making bread, pizza, hot dogs and cinnamon rolls. She took over when I forgot to take cakes out of the oven.

I stood with her while she demonstrated how to make yoghurt. We laughed as I wobbled on a precarious chair, reaching up to put tubs of home-made yoghurt on our hot tin roof to allow them to incubate. Once Jane had gone home, the other challenge for me was remembering to get the yoghurt down in the dusky evening.

Our milk was delivered on weekday mornings by a Tanzanian neighbour. He kept cows and was pleased to sell us their milk, which had to be boiled to eliminate dangerous brucellosis bacteria. Jane would carefully sieve the fresh cow's milk into a vast saucepan and then drop in an old saucer, before placing it on the stove and lighting the gas flame. When I first arrived in Dodoma, I wondered aloud why Jane put a saucer into the pan with the milk. It soon became apparent that its rattle indicated when the milk was starting to boil. Despite this rudimentary warning system, I frequently left it too late and the boiled milk started to overflow. Ugh! The dreadful smell of burnt milk – and the waste of milk after all that effort.

One morning, our cat turned up her feline nose and refused to touch the unusually yellow, tainted milk. The next day, I decided to question the milkman in my best Swahili before his hasty retreat: 'What happened to yesterday's milk? It was very bad. We could not drink it.'

'Mmmm…' He sought to evade the question.

'The milk was bad – why?' I tried again.

'Yesterday, the cow put her foot in the bucket – but not today, Mama Esther, not today!'

I was getting used to being addressed as the mother of my oldest child, but I wasn't so used to tales of cows placing filthy hooves in our milk. I would have to be more vigilant with checking the milk. Thankfully, the cow behaved herself better after that.

My next challenge was learning to prepare fresh meat. It arrived at our house, swilling in blood, fresh from its slaughter at the meat market. However, I was grateful that I didn't have to attend the slaughter. Instead, my friend's house lady, Elizabeti, fetched the meat for me. When Elizabeti delivered the sun-warmed bucket on a Saturday afternoon, Ben loved to stand on a stool to help me wash the meat. I used water diluted with Milton to kill any germs. I braced myself as I extracted the meat from inches of tepid animal blood, but nothing made Ben squeamish! I love the photograph that captures Ben's beaming smile as he purposefully rinsed our cuts of beef, chicken or pork.

All that remained was the dividing, bagging and freezing of the meat. Apparently, freezing fresh meat destroyed any potential parasites that might want to hatch in our brains or stomachs. I'd heard revolting tales of worm invasion that I didn't want repeated in my family.

Four years of domestic exposure in Dodoma paid off. I accrued cooking skills I never could have imagined when living a life of culinary ease in London. I pull down my recipe books today and smile. Flicking through their familiar pages, I know I can confidently prepare many of these dishes – and I am thankful for the way God gave me abilities I didn't expect, from a country I never expected to live in.

15
A stressful departure

Esther climbed aboard the MAF minibus with four other MAF kids, her blonde hair tied in a neat ponytail. It was not yet 7.30 a.m., but it was time for them to set off for the twenty-minute drive to Canon Andrea Mwaka School. Daily life starts early in Africa. Esther held tightly on to her pink backpack and stretched her four-year-old legs to climb up the steep step. Once seated, she waved through the window, smiling happily. The mums took it in turns to drive the children; this was my morning off and I relished the free time ahead.

It was a crisp, bright day, perfect for some exercise. I called Ben, who was busy filling his yellow, plastic digger with stones from the garden's empty flower bed. When he toddled over, I lifted him into the carrier seat on the back of my bicycle. Cycling was pleasant on the side roads because Dodoma is so flat. In contrast, cycling in town was not so enjoyable, even though there wasn't much traffic, because cars rarely made allowances for bicycles. I therefore resolved to be extra careful on the main road through town.

Ben and I had an easy ride and stopped at the Two Sisters shop – a small but well-stocked, Indian-owned food store, the closest thing we had to a supermarket in town. I felt hungry, so I bought a bag of potato chips to share with Ben before we mounted my bike for our ride home. Ben was a great passenger, sitting behind me and taking in all the sights and sounds of the dusty Tanzanian streets.

When we got home, I unstrapped Ben from his seat, then suddenly felt queasy. After I just made it to the bathroom in time to vomit into the toilet, Jane came through from the kitchen looking concerned. *'Habari yako, mama?'* ('How are you, ma'am?') she asked. *'Una kikohozi?'* ('Do you have a cough?')

I looked at Jane and decided to tell her the truth. *'Hapana, Jane. Nina mimba!'* ('No, Jane. I'm pregnant!')

'Bwana asifiwe!' ('Praise the Lord!') she cried, a smile breaking across her usually serious-looking face.

The morning sickness thankfully eased after a few weeks – but being pregnant in Dodoma made me feel extra warm, all the time! As my stomach grew bigger, I was so uncomfortably sweltering in my Western clothes that I decided to ditch them. Instead, I opted for the long, flowing dresses they sold in town, which were like enormous tents. They were unflattering, but oh-so comfy. When I was given a bright-orange tent-dress at a Tanzanian graduation ceremony, I decided to start wearing it. Orange isn't a good colour on me, especially when enveloping my entire body. The spectacular robe was trimmed with gold lace that glinted in the sunlight, far more glitzy than my normal clothes. However, it didn't matter to me how I looked – I just wanted to feel comfortable.

One afternoon, when it was my turn to drive to school to pick up the MAF kids, I was wearing my orange tent. I climbed down from the minibus, then floated over to the sandy playground, a vision of colour.

'Who *is* that bright, round, tangerine creature?' asked my friend's husband.

'That, darling, is Liz!' replied Sharon.

I couldn't wait to get back to the cooler weather of England – and hopefully wear more conventional maternity clothes. Andrew and I had decided it would be wise to have the baby back in Lancashire to be close to family. That way, we could combine the baby's arrival with our MAF home assignment. This was a chance to visit supporting churches and friends and give them feedback about our work – and would be our first visit to England since arriving in Dodoma eighteen months earlier. We looked forward to sharing photos, videos and stories to demonstrate how their generous giving had helped the people of Tanzania.

I planned to leave Tanzania with Esther and Ben a few weeks earlier than Andrew so that I could get ready for the baby's birth. Andrew would drive us all to Dar es Salaam (a nine-hour drive), where we would all stay overnight, then see us off at the airport the next morning before driving straight back to Dodoma to continue his work. The children and I were excited at the prospect of time with grandparents. I looked forward to a trouble-free birth in the friendly, efficient hospital where Esther had been born. Andrew would then join us just before the baby's due date.

Dar es Salaam's heat is overwhelming, its humidity wrapping around you like a wet embrace. On the day of our departure, I staggered into Dar es Salaam's International Airport, clinging to the sweaty hand of three-year-old Ben and keeping a careful eye on Esther, who recently turned five. I was around thirty-four weeks pregnant and felt overheated even as we entered the air-conditioned lobby. Strict rules at Dar es Salaam airport meant that only passengers were allowed into the departure hall. I was apprehensive. What if Andrew could not come to help me check in, with my enormous, heavy belly and two excited little ones?

Thankfully, Andrew was wearing his pilot's uniform that morning. Each shoulder of his blue shirt bore four golden stripes, shouting a loud message to the airport officials. Recognising his MAF uniform, they gave him permission to enter past security and assist his pregnant wife. This was a welcome answer to my prayers. It was a relief to have Andrew's strong arms to help shift luggage on and off the security belts and trolleys, to haul suitcases and to watch our energetic children while I checked in.

It was a tearful farewell for me as I hugged Andrew goodbye. I consciously ignored the stares of other passengers and the Tanzanian airport staff. Then, wiping away my tears, I resolutely picked up our hand luggage. A trickle of sweat made its way down my back as I bent over to help Esther pick up her travel bag, packed with toys and games to occupy her and Ben on the long flight. With my spare hand I grabbed Ben and steered us towards the official emigration desk. It was time to have our passports stamped for departure.

Travelling alone with small children made me anxious. The weight of my yet-to-be-born baby was matched by the extra weight of responsibility I felt and I kept a careful eye on both Esther and Ben, not daring to relax for a moment. We joined the queue and I shuffled the children along until we reached the emigration desk. Absently, I passed our three passports through the small disc-shaped window, expecting them to be quickly stamped and returned.

I was surprised when the normally simple process took longer than a few minutes. Leaning in towards the window, I was taken aback to encounter a stern frown furrowing the brow of the official behind the desk.

'Madame, your visa has expired,' he began.

Shocked, I was lost for words. The sombre face of the emigration officer told me he was not in the least bit amused.

'You cannot leave Tanzania with an expired visa. It is a punishable offence…'

Another quick scan told me that Esther and Ben were still close, but I could feel my palms becoming sweaty as I asked to look at the visa page in my passport. Horror of horrors, he was correct! My visa was dependent on Andrew's work permit. When Andrew's permit had been updated, we had not realised that my passport needed a new stamp too. It was a basic administrative oversight – but the consequences suddenly seemed scary.

In an instant, my expectations of baby Parker arriving in an English hospital, with my parents and friends nearby, vanished like a popped balloon. Instead, a wildly dramatic image filled my mind. I pictured myself locked in a dark cell in a hostile Tanzanian prison, about to give birth to my baby on the dirty earth floor of a jail. I pictured my two hungry children crouching nearby, full of fear as I shouted for help. I could almost hear the squeak of dreaded rats and the cries of fellow prisoners. Imagination is a powerful tool – and at this moment, mine was super-powered.

The official's hard stare brought me back to reality. I realised with a rush of hope that Andrew might still be nearby – surely if Andrew's up-to-date visa was presented, the issue could be solved? I fumbled in my bag for my phone and asked the official if he would kindly consider talking to my husband, whose visa I was dependent on? My heart was beating fast. I was close to tears. Confrontations with administrative staff in a foreign airport can be stressful at the best of times, but with my journey now in jeopardy and my baby due to arrive in a few weeks, the pressure was mounting.

I made a frantic call to Andrew. Happily, he was still in the airport and soon appeared next to us. He took one look at my agitated expression and steered me towards a yellow line painted on the airport floor. 'Stay here,' he ordered gently, but firmly. 'Don't move off this line. Don't say a word!'

He knows me so well. I didn't trust myself not to say something rash and unhelpful. I called Esther and Ben to stand with me and tried to distract them while my South African husband stepped forward, his passport at the ready, his visa visible and his calm face in place. I sent up hasty prayers, asking God to give the official extra grace to pardon our mistake.

It was several minutes and many humble apologies later before the emigration officer was satisfied. He could see that Andrew's permit was valid, thus affording me the legal right to be in Tanzania. He accepted that there had been a genuine error in the paperwork – but we needed to rectify it immediately. Plans were put in place to pay the fee and sort out the problem, with the help of MAF. Thankfully, the official knew MAF and trusted their excellent reputation. When he finally granted me permission to leave, I was immensely grateful. The ink from the exit stamp was still fresh when I swooped on my passport and hastily bid a second farewell to Andrew. I guided the children through the barrier as quickly as I could, keen to get on that plane to Manchester before the official could change his mind.

I boarded our Emirates flight with great relief! After settling Esther and Ben either side of my seat, I and my huge stomach got comfortable. I adjusted our pillows and thanked God for His help in this stressful departure from Tanzania. It had been a close call.

16

Quicker than expected

Esther, Ben and I were enjoying our few weeks with my parents before the arrival of the baby. Baby's due date was still a little over three weeks away, and Andrew was not due to come to England for at least another two weeks. Our baby, though, had other plans, as I discovered when my waters broke early...

'Mum?' I hissed into the darkness. 'MUM!' It was no use. Her body needed to sleep and no amount of calling was going to wake her at this hour. She was feeling uncharacteristically poorly with a nasty chest infection. Normally active and determined, my mum was now forced to her bed. At night, she was knocked out by strong medication to combat the illness, which transported her to a land of deep dreams. I couldn't wake her up.

Nor did I want to want to wake Esther and Ben, who were enjoying blissful sleep in their bedroom down the corridor, snugly tucked into bunkbeds.

I stood uncertain in the darkness, holding open the door to my parents' bedroom. It was only 3 a.m. and it seemed unfair to wake them if I could wait a little longer.

Instead, I tiptoed to the spare room, turned on the computer and opened up Skype. Oh good, there was enough credit on our Skype account to make a call to an overseas mobile number. I dialled Andrew's number in Tanzania, knowing that it was already 6 a.m. there. Since it was a work day, I expected Andrew to be up and dressed to prepare for his MAF flight.

Andrew answered quickly. I felt strangely relaxed as I asked him how he was, but he was suspicious. Why would I call him so early in the morning, which meant it was still night in Britain? 'Are you OK, my love?' he asked.

'Well,' I said, 'I am OK, but my waters have broken – and I'm really sorry, but I don't think you're going to make it back here in time for our baby's delivery.'

I paused while a mild contraction distracted me.

'I think I still have some time, but not enough for you to get here before his arrival,' I continued.

Andrew, normally the dependably calm one, sounded uptight. 'Are you sure? What if it's a false alarm?' he ventured, hopefully.

I *was* sure. After all, this was my third baby. I felt surprisingly collected as I measured the fairly long gaps between my contractions. At least this time I wasn't sitting at a road block in South Africa! Ormskirk Hospital was just twenty minutes down the road in the car and I was already registered on their system. Thanks to an efficient midwife I had met a few days previously, all of my paperwork was in order and a scan three days earlier had shown that the baby was in just the right position for an easy birth. Feeling like God had put all the right details in place reassured me that the baby's arrival would go smoothly – and would keep me uncharacteristically calm through my labour.

However, I had not expected to go into labour so much earlier than the due date. Just a few days ago, I had visited my friend Wendy, whose house was a short drive from my parents' home. Wendy and I joked about the possibility of my baby arriving before Andrew got to England. I confidently stated that Andrew had to make it to Lancashire in time. Wendy laughed with me at my easy confidence, but also told me, 'Liz, honestly, *if* the baby does come before Andrew, please call me. I'll come to the hospital with you – that's a promise.'

Now, as I sat talking to Andrew in far-off Tanzania, I remembered Wendy's promise. I reassured Andrew that I would call Wendy if need be. He was glad to hear it. After chatting for a few more minutes, Andrew had to hang up and prepare for his busy day, flying a medical flight. We said goodbye and I switched off the Skype call.

I went downstairs to eat a bowl of cereal. I was ravenous and far too wide awake to sleep. By 5 a.m., the contractions were coming faster. I packed an overnight bag, then phoned the hospital for advice.

'Well, love, if the contractions are less than five minutes apart, then just come into the maternity ward.' The nurse on the other end of the phone was so relaxed about the matter that she added to the composure I already felt.

I thought I had better try again to waken my parents – or at least my dad. 'Dad! Dad, I need to go to the hospital – the baby is coming!'

There was a loud grunt, then the silhouette of my dad's dishevelled hair appeared outlined in the darkness. He sat up suddenly in panic. *'What?'* Alarmed, Dad sprang into action, leaping out of bed, confused and alert all at the same time, knocking into the furniture in his rush to get up.

Despite the initial panic, Dad was fantastic. He managed to wake Mum enough to make her understand that he was taking me to hospital. He explained that he hoped to be back in time to help Esther and Ben get up and have their breakfast, then drive Esther to school. Esther was attending a local primary school for a few weeks while we were in England.

I went back downstairs and picked up the landline to call Wendy. By now, it was 5.30 a.m. and the first rays of sunlight were starting to pierce the dull darkness of this March morning. Wendy answered quickly. Despite the earliness of my call, she was as helpful as my dad, assuring me that she would meet me at the hospital as soon as possible.

I picked up my overnight bag and moved towards the front door. Mum had now woken up. Feeling groggy but worried, she came downstairs in her dressing gown to wave us off. As we opened the front door, the milkman's van was trundling down the otherwise deserted street, piled high with jingling glass bottles. Surprised to have company at dawn, the milkman greeted us warmly but curiously. I gave him a cheery wave while Dad explained that he was taking me to hospital for my baby to be born.

The milkman nearly fell out of his van. He turned to my mum and commented, 'She looks so calm, it's like she's just popping out to the shops!' I smiled. I knew that the peace I felt did not come from me, but was because I could see God working out the details for the baby's arrival, even when my greatest support, my husband, was away in a distant land.

That early-morning drive to Ormskirk Hospital was unforgettable. Dad was terrified in case I had the baby in his car. He tried to distract us both all the way there, talking of all things about the crop rotation system of Lancashire farming! I half-listened, growing increasingly uncomfortable, kneeling up on the back seat and praying fervently that I would NOT have this baby by the side of the road but would make it to the hospital in time.

And we did. Dad accompanied me in the nearest lift up to the maternity ward, the night porter laughing with us when he realised that this seventy-year-old man was unusually the grandfather, not the father, of the baby about to be born. Despite the effort to speak between contractions, I briefly told him that my baby's dad was working in Africa.

I was ushered through the doors of the maternity ward at 6.10 a.m. Dad passed me to the capable hands of the midwives – and dashed away as fast as his legs would carry him. By 6.19 a.m., I was sitting on a hospital bed with my baby son in my arms, overjoyed as I looked down at this precious bundle of love.

Joel Matthew had safely arrived to join our family.

Wendy arrived just minutes after Joel's birth, bringing with her a very welcome dose of friendship plus thoughtful bags of baby clothes and nappies. 'Chris packed some breakfast for you, Liz,' she added, handing me a paper bag full of treats from her husband. Then tucking her long, blonde hair behind her ears, she bent down to get a closer look at baby Joel. Smiling, she reached for a cuddle with my new-born son. I smiled back and carefully handed Joel over to meet his future godmother. Thanks to Wendy, Joel now had clothes to wear. I had not been back in England long enough to do a proper shopping trip, so Joel's surprisingly early arrival meant an unprepared mother.

Shortly afterwards, Wendy rummaged in my bag and pulled out my phone. I needed to call Andrew and tell him the great news. It was an emotional call. I was ecstatic – but Andrew was so far away. I missed him – and felt bad for him. His voice was choked when he heard how quickly Joel had arrived. 'I wish I was with you both,' he said wistfully. Suddenly, Tanzania seemed even further away than before.

Even though Andrew could not yet be by my side, I was not alone. Wendy stayed with me through the critical health checks and formalities. After Wendy left, it 'just so happened' that my sister-in-law Jenny, an occupational therapist, was working a shift at the hospital, so she popped into my ward. 'Oh, Liz,' she exclaimed, as she looked down at her tiny nephew. Jenny cradled Joel in her arms and shed a few compassionate tears, conscious that Joel had yet to be held by his dad. God was lining up people to offer support – in the right place, at the right time.

Later that morning, I texted my brother and asked him to bring the cot from his house to our parents' home, since Joel had nowhere to sleep once we got out of hospital. My dad came back to hospital that same afternoon. His kind face broke out in a huge smile as he met his latest grandson. He brought Esther and Ben with him to meet their baby brother. It was a delightful scene. They took turns to cuddle Joel, simultaneously intrigued and proud.

The next day, I was discharged. Dad drove me and Joel to my parents' home. I was amazed as so many caring people rallied round and even dropped off meals. Baby items, cute outfits, cards, chocolates and flowers kept arriving. My phone constantly buzzed with happy messages of congratulations and support from Tanzania. I was delighted to receive a text message in Swahili from my house lady Jane, who too was looking forward to meeting Joel. My heart was full of gratitude for the love shown by so many.

The best gift for Joel arrived on Friday evening: his Dad! It was quite the journey for this father to come and meet his new-born son. Andrew had received my call about

Joel's birth in Mbeya, in south-west Tanzania. Thanks to an understanding colleague, he was instantly taken off flight duty and instead flew home to Dodoma, where Andrew packed his bags and prepared to shut up our house for the next few weeks. Early the following morning, he drove to Dar es Salaam, stayed overnight with hospitable MAF friends and then boarded Friday morning's flight to Manchester. He finally landed in Lancashire on Friday evening, after a three-day journey from one continent to another! As soon as Andrew stepped into the house, our family felt complete again. Andrew smiled from ear to ear as he finally met his baby son.

Two days later, we moved into a pretty canal-side apartment belonging to our friend Lara, not too far from my parents. Then followed a hectic few weeks of leading MAF meetings, visiting churches to talk about Andrew's work and catching up on vaccinations and paperwork. We also took time to visit Andrew's parents at the house they had retired to on the Isle of Wight. It was a happy period with family and we consciously made the most of every minute until we had to go back overseas. We had already received Joel's passport. He was so tiny at just a few weeks old that we could barely wake him for the photograph, but now we that we had his paperwork in place, our return to Tanzania felt closer.

Joel had just turned eleven weeks old when we strapped him into his car seat and gently placed him next to his brother and sister in an extra-large taxi organised by generous friends. Our twelve suitcases were loaded into the back of the vehicle, bursting at the seams with clothes and shoes for the children to last the next eighteen months, advance Christmas and birthday gifts, baby gear, medicine supplies, Marmite, Oxo cubes and vials of vaccines for Joel. The wheels of the taxi started to roll; we were on course to take Joel to his first African home.

The goodbyes never get easier, so I made sure tissues were in my hand luggage. When we went through Manchester Airport this time, it wasn't just Mum and I who needed the tissues. Esther, at five years old, was learning the process of greetings and goodbyes. The tears came thick and fast down her young cheeks as she wrapped her arms around her grandparents in farewell. I choked back my own tears so that I could comfort Esther, silently acknowledging that my daughter was already experienced with the rollercoaster cycle of arrivals and farewells.

We settled at last into our airline seats for our long-haul flight. As the aircraft lights were dimmed and the children dozed, I reflected back on the last few weeks. We had received so much kindness; we had seen people appear in just the right place and exactly when we needed them. My baby arrived earlier than expected, but God still worked out every detail. I knew without a doubt that He would continue to lead us back into Africa, whatever may lie ahead.

17

Night-time health scares

My heart was beating fast, adrenaline was coursing through my body, causing me to stay awake despite the heaviness of my eyes in this dead of night. My baby son lay next to me, his chest rising and falling with alarming speed. His baby lips were tinged with blue. I placed my ears next to his chest again to check, but the rasping breathing had not gone away. Then came the barking cough once more. I resumed my prayers that I would know what to do and that God would spare baby Joel, leading me to help in the morning.

I reached for the computer, read about croup and found medical websites full of information. However, with no option to call a doctor at this time of night, I was reluctant to try remedies that might worsen the situation. Sleep was elusive: fervent prayer was my only recourse. I was learning a whole new level of prayer in Dodoma, waiting for God to act.

As the muted colours of dawn filtered through my mosquito net, I thanked God that Joel was still breathing and responsive. Hauling myself out of bed, I wondered who to ring. The American doctor we knew in Magumbua, the village we had visited with Andrew on the MAF plane, came to mind. Although it was a few hours away by road and mobile-phone coverage there could be temperamental, I decided to call him for advice.

Dr John Eager answered quickly, to my immense relief. He seemed surprised to be answering a call, but not as amazed as I was when he explained that he was at a medical conference with his phone switched to mute. He had literally just stepped outside to check for calls. It was that perfect timing which can only be worked out by the Lord.

John is as gracious and as kind a doctor as you could hope to meet. He listened carefully to my description of Joel's symptoms and recommended salbutamol tablets to relieve the breathing troubles and an antibiotic to ease what sounded like a chest infection. These were easily available in Dodoma, where medicines can be purchased over the counter without prescriptions. Over the next few days, Joel's health was restored.

In Dodoma, there were several other health incidents with Joel, and these seemed to begin as soon as Andrew flew away on trips. From our bedroom, I could watch the MAF planes emerge from behind the hangar, rising high into the blue African sky. Often, the plane would be carrying Andrew away for a few days with a busy schedule – for example, when he flew Elisha and other Masai evangelists in Malambo, northern Tanzania into hard-to-reach villages. I would anxiously check Joel's temperature when the red and white aeroplane faded to a small dot in the sky, nervous in case he fell ill again while his dad was away.

On one such occasion, Joel came down with another chest infection and an unusually high fever. I had already been to DCMC (Dodoma Christian Medical Centre) in the morning. The duty doctor had given me antibiotics for Joel's chest infection, but they weren't stopping his fever from climbing higher. I began to feel the familiar concern, but I didn't want to drag three small children to the draughty DCMC once again. Besides, doctor visits could take an inordinately *long* time in Dodoma. It was a twenty-minute drive on an uneven, gravelly road up the isolated hill to spend the evening –and maybe even the night – waiting to see a doctor and then waiting even longer for test results. In the end, I decided to carry Joel across the compound and out into the neighbourhood to visit a small local clinic.

It was almost dusk when I slipped across the road with my baby. I entered through the dark doorway and explained to the pharmacist how hot Joel felt. The staff agreed to carry out a rapid malaria test. A young Tanzanian lady rubbed an alcohol wipe across Joel's fingers and pricked one with a sharp lancet to draw blood – causing Joel to yelp. She then placed a long, thin pipette against the wound, to suck up Joel's blood, before squeezing it to empty his blood into a round well on a plastic malaria test. Opening a small bottle of clear liquid, she added this to another round well on the test. 'Call after fifteen minutes and we will give you the results,' she instructed me. I was grateful that she had carried out the test so efficiently. I hated trying to get blood out of the children myself when we attempted these tests at home.

When I rang back, I was told the test was positive. I was horrified; my heart sank. Malaria can be such a frightening word. Joel was only seven months old; he seemed so vulnerable. His positive test result sent me into a spin. Anxiety struck its way into my heart and into my hands. I felt unable to function normally. I asked someone to cross the road and pick up the anti-malaria pills, but felt lost with the looming responsibility of caring alone for my sick baby, far from a reliable hospital or trusted doctor. Andrew was away for two nights in Malambo. In those days, Malambo had no mobile phone tower, so he was uncontactable.

Esther and Ben sat disconsolately at our large, wooden dining table. They gazed without enthusiasm at their dinner: a bowl of Weetabix. This was all I could manage to serve – something that needed no heating up. Subdued, they watched me with wide eyes as I hurried about the house, trying to calm their fretful baby brother. Even many years later, Esther still reminds me, 'That was the night I put my tooth under my pillow but the tooth fairy didn't come!'

One of the huge blessings of our life with MAF has always been the caring community around us. Living on our compound was a gifted nurse from Germany, who ran a remarkable ministry with street kids. Andrea came to the rescue, checking Joel's results at the clinic, cross-checking the dosage of Joel's medicine and reassuring me about how to administer the pills to such a small baby. She reminded me that I could call on her again if Joel got worse. I knew Andrea was dependable. After all, she had stitched up Esther's bleeding head when she fell off the climbing frame and superglued the skin of Ben's split chin together when he came crashing off a swing onto a concrete floor.

Across town, Andrew's sister Claire was busy with her classroom preparations. Happily, she had moved to Dodoma in 2010 and worked as a teacher at Canon Andrea Mwaka Primary School, where Esther and Ben both attended. Still frantic, I called her asking for help. Very graciously, Claire came to stay overnight, helping to settle Esther and Ben and make tea for this frazzled mother. At 3 a.m., I shook a tired Claire awake. 'Claire,' I whispered into the dim night, tying not to wake the sleeping children. 'Can you please help me give Joel his next dose of Coartem? I can't manage on my own.'

These little yellow anti-malaria tablets had to be given at fixed intervals, crushed into a spoonful of breast milk for my unweaned baby. It was a messy business: expressing milk into a teaspoon, mixing it with the pill, forcing the spoon into a protesting baby's mouth and all in the unsociable darkness of the early hours of the morning. Claire had to get up again just three hours later to make her way back across Dodoma and be ready in her classroom before her students arrived. Her selfless assistance meant the world to me. Once again, God provided help just when I needed it.

Andrew returned home two days later. In his blue MAF shirt, clutching his flight bag and tired from a long, hot flight, he entered the cool of our house, no doubt expecting the usual noisy welcome of boisterous kids and perhaps a cup of tea from his wife. Instead, he heard how high Joel's fever had been and how Auntie Claire had to come to stay. Andrew looked in disbelief at baby Joel, now happily playing on the red, concrete floor, and commented, 'No, they must have got the diagnosis wrong. He looks fine to me!'

I shot Andrew a look of incredulity and insisted how unwell his tiny son had been.

Yes, Joel did look fine now. He quickly bounced back from his malaria. The Coartem had worked wonders. The antibiotics were working well too – but this calm scene belied the drama which reigned a few days earlier in Andrew's absence. How thankful I was for God's placing of people around me at just the right time. While Andrew was often away overnight in our Dodoma years, I was never alone: I was surrounded and provided for by the One who always remains close.

18

A cathedral celebration

A few days before Joel was about to celebrate his first birthday, Andrew drove to Dar es Salaam – and returned home with a very special present. As he drew up to the MAF compound car park in our large Prado, the doors flew open and Joel's grandparents – my parents – emerged. Andrew had fetched them from their flight and they were ready for a nice cup of tea after their long journey by air and road.

Mum was thrilled to be back in East Africa. It wasn't her beloved Uganda, but Tanzania was one step closer. She soon observed that twenty-first-century Dodoma was not modern by British standards, but was far more contemporary than 1960s Karamoja. After a few days, I noticed that she stopped trying to compare Dodoma to Kotido. Instead, she took in the new experiences around her, as she and Dad got a three-week glimpse of our

Tanzanian life. For Dad, this was his first taste of East Africa. When he left, he wrote in our visitors' book, 'What a wonderful time together!'

The children were delighted to share their Dodoma life with grandparents for the first time. Their young voices rang out as they showed Nana and Grandad their house, their school, their friends, the MAF compound and its swimming pool.

Mum and Dad were honoured when Mama Kambenga generously invited them to come and eat a Tanzanian meal at her home. Joel sat proudly on Mama Kambenga's knee as we sampled traditional dishes: *ugali*, *nyama choma*, *pilau*. Mama Kambenga had a soft spot for Joel, since he joined us during my language lessons. *'Rafiki yangu'* ('my friend') she called him. She spoke impeccable English and my parents enjoyed asking her questions about Tanzanian life.

Mum and I joined Mama Kambenga one morning to visit a local nursery school that she helped to oversee. The basic school building had few windows and the tiny children sat crammed on rough wooden benches lined up across the dark room, where they learnt by rote from their teachers. The only adornment on the concrete walls was a simple blackboard. It was a world away from the well-resourced, hands-on classroom environment where my mum had recently worked as a nursery teacher in Liverpool.

On their second Sunday, we had an extra special event lined up. We had been given special permission for my dad, an ordained Anglican minister, to lead a Service of

Thanksgiving for Joel at Dodoma Anglican Cathedral. This was the church we attended as a family.

Dodoma cathedral, set in a dry, sandy compound off the main road, was an unusual design. Its large bricks wore a greyish tinge in the dust and its distinctive round dome sat proudly on top of the hexagonal building. A tall stone cross was perched on the centre of the dome, announcing the faith of its congregation to the people of the city. On Sundays, crowds of people flocked to worship at the cathedral, wearing their best clothes. The colourful display of gathered Tanzanian worshippers was visually stunning. Most people came for the Swahili-language services, and as the crowds pushed into the large church, there was barely space to slide into a pew. While the services took place, we might find a goat tethered outside or chickens wandering about. These were the live gifts offered as a tithe to God, instead of money. It was one of these chickens that once chased a terrified Ben down the aisle of the church during a Sunday morning service, clucking furiously as my son raced away and making everyone laugh.

Our family usually attended the English-speaking services, with a much smaller congregation, but this Sunday there were extra faces seated on the wooden pews as several of our friends came to join Joel's thanksgiving service. It was a warm morning, so I was thankful for the light breeze as our family was invited up to the front of the church. As we stood in that airy, domed, stone cathedral in Tanzania's capital city, Dad's voice echoed clearly. Next, Claire prayed a special prayer for her nephew and godson.

That morning, Joel was wearing a smart, blue, patterned shirt made for him by one of my Tanzanian seamstress friends, with material from Dodoma market. I was wearing a locally made outfit too. As I looked around, I noticed what a startling scene we presented. There were my parents from England. There was my husband and his sister. Perched on the church pews were our international MAF team and local friends from Tanzania. I saw England merging with Tanzania and South Africa, and with Switzerland, America, Australia and New Zealand. Here we were, giving thanks for Joel; a multi-national group praying to the same God. Our God is above all borders. It was beautiful.

Afterwards, our friends, neighbours and MAF colleagues joined us in our garden for tea, coffee and cake. An American friend, who worked for SIL Bible Translators, had baked the most stunning of cakes for Joel. Our children and their friends ran here, there and everywhere, enjoying a happy playtime. The excited sounds of their games added to the hum of adult conversation. It was a true celebration.

As I tidied away later that afternoon and put an overtired Joel in bed for his afternoon nap, I thought again what a rare day it had been. As a child, I had attended countless church services that my dad had led – but always in England and mostly in Liverpool. I don't think any of us could have imagined my dad leading a service in a Tanzanian cathedral, especially a service for a grandson growing up in Africa. I was amazed that my wild promise to God to 'go anywhere' for Him had brought me – and now my parents – all the way to Tanzania. However, I didn't yet realise that Tanzania was simply one step on a longer road – a journey that would take us further than we thought possible.

19

'I'm not taking my family to a war zone'

God of Justice, Saviour to all
Came to rescue the weak and the poor
Came to serve and not be served
And Jesus, You have called us
Freely we've received now freely we will give
We must go, live to feed the hungry
Stand beside the broken, we must go
Stepping forward keep us from just singing
Move us into action, we must go
Fill us up, send us out…

The music and lyrics of this Tim Hughes song rang out through my Dodoma lounge. Joel was busy toddling about, cute in his denim dungarees. Jane was pottering happily in the kitchen, the warm aroma of fresh-baked *sconzi* (bread rolls) drifting through our home. Esther and Ben were at school and Andrew had a busy day of flying.

Outside, the Tanzanian sun lit up the spiky, dry grass of our garden. The bougainvillea climbing over our dark green hedge boasted startling red and purple flowers, dancing merrily in the light breeze. It was a beautiful morning.

Our days had settled into a straightforward rhythm. Dodoma was the only way of life my children remembered and it felt normal to them. But perhaps we were too settled?

Something started to stir in my soul and the words of the song began to chafe as I tried to sing along. Could I honestly say that I was prepared to go somewhere else? Could I start again, 'stepping forward' to a new venture? Could I 'stand beside the broken' wherever God would send us? Or was I simply singing without sincerity? Was I becoming stuck in a rut that was feeling more and more controllable the longer we lived here?

What if I really let God have control? Could I trust Him to 'move us into action' even if that meant another place, or perhaps a return to England where strong family ties beckoned us back?

We were heading towards the end of 2013. We had completed four years in Tanzania with MAF and Andrew's contract was coming to an end. We could renew it, but where? Andrew was keen to train on the larger planes, the fourteen-seater Cessna Caravan 208, which were no longer flown out of Dodoma. Also, there was talk within MAF that the Tanzania programme would become significantly smaller as the country's infrastructure became more developed. That was a positive step forward for Tanzania, but left us MAF staff with a growing sense of uncertainty.

Andrew and I decided to do what we had done back in London in 2004, almost ten years earlier: pray. We prayed very specifically, asking the Lord if He was leading us somewhere else. We asked Him to show us the next step as a family. Next, we talked to MAF about the possibility of moving to another programme, another country.

That is when strange things started to happen.

MAF offered us two possibilities where Cessna Caravan pilot positions were available. The first position was in Papua New Guinea. That sounded exotic and exciting! The second was in South Sudan. Andrew and I looked at each other, smiling wryly.

'South Sudan?' quipped Andrew, 'I'm not taking my family to a war zone!' We dismissed the idea as outrageous.

We started to look up information and blog posts from MAF families based in Papua New Guinea. We tried to get enthusiastic. We tried to picture ourselves packing up to move there, to be involved in MAF's work in that mountainous country – but no matter how hard we tried, the spark to motivate us just wouldn't ignite…

That's when my mum called us on Skype to tell us that she had watched a MAF video about the work in South Sudan – and that the South Sudan programme manager presenting the video was Bastiaan de Waal, whom my parents had met with us at our MAF training in 2009. Mum was excited to have watched a video by someone we all knew. It seemed odd to me, though, that it was about South Sudan – Mum had no idea that MAF had mentioned to us the possibility of working there.

One Sunday evening shortly afterwards, Andrew and I got the three little Parkers happily settled in their beds, then decided to listen to a sermon podcast from our old church, St Michael's in London. *Oh good,* I thought, sinking into our soft sofa after a busy, hot day. *It will be nice to hear the familiar voice of our vicar Charles and listen to his excellent teaching.*

Andrew rigged up the computer and the downloaded sermon began to play. It was a typical Dodoma evening: hot and dry. But wait a minute… Why was I suddenly feeling cold and clammy? Why did I have goosebumps running up and down my arm? The speaker being broadcast into our African lounge, from far-off London, was not the expected voice of Charles Marnham. Instead, it was a visiting speaker from International Justice Mission – and all I could hear were his words that he had just been in *South Sudan,* helping the Christians there to stand up for their Christian faith. I remembered nothing else of his talk, but looked at Andrew in wonder, asking why this country which I had never really thought much about was now popping up unexpectedly and becoming hard to ignore?

A few days later, my precious friend Sarah popped by for a cup of tea. Sunny and bright, her personality matched the happy morning sunshine of that Dodoma day. I heard her friendly greeting before I saw her. She swirled her way into our lounge with a huge smile, her blonde hair lit up by the sunlight, her dress of pretty pink flowing freely around her ankles. 'Hi Liz, I've just had *the best* news! My friend from my home church, Esther, is coming to visit us here in Dodoma.' British-born Sarah, like me, missed her English friends, so this was fantastic news for her.

'That's great!' I responded.

But before I could continue, Sarah added, 'She works in an orphanage in Africa and will be getting the bus from the country where she is now based...'

I suddenly had a deep instinct about where this Esther currently worked. 'Don't tell me, Sarah – she's been living in South Sudan, hasn't she?'

Sarah looked at me in astonishment. 'How did you know that?'

'Well...' I started to explain how I knew, but found myself crumbling into tears. This simply could not be another coincidence. God was trying to tell me something. I felt like I could no longer deny the call that seemed to be for me and my family.

A concerned Sarah rushed across the floor of our lounge and to the dining table where I had just set down mugs of tea. I was reaching for kitchen towel to dry my eyes. 'What's wrong, Liz?' she gently asked.

'I think God is calling us to South Sudan,' I replied.

'Oh, Liz!' she said. From this brief response, I knew that my friend understood my conflicting emotions. She understood my sadness about leaving Tanzania, my excitement for new adventures and also the fear of the unknown.

South Sudan was renowned for its legacy of war and conflict – and this made me fearful. How could we keep a young family safe in such a place? How could a war-torn country have good medical and education facilities for my growing family?

Sarah looked as concerned as I felt, but her solution was wise. She took my hand to pray for me, committing my fears to God. She asked God for clarity about this call to a new country; a call which seemed to be getting louder every day. I was so grateful for her unselfish support. It is hard to lose a friend when living overseas, but despite the sad possibility of us parting company which now lay ahead, Sarah simply asked for God's will for my family.

In my own times with God, I asked Him over and over whether I had heard right and honestly told Him my fears. One morning, the Lord showed me this passage: 'Fear of man will prove to be a snare, but whoever trusts in the LORD is kept safe' (Proverbs 29:25).

This provided reassurance for my scared soul. I had been busy telling the Lord that I was fearful of fighting men. He, in turn, was reminding me that instead I should be fixing my eyes on Him, since He has ultimate control of my safety. As I trusted Him, He was promising to keep us safe. I felt myself take a step towards saying 'yes' to South Sudan.

Andrew came home later that day. He stood across from me, his shoulders sagging. I could tell he felt tired and harried. MAF needed a decision, but we were still weighing up whether we could commit to leaving Tanzania for South Sudan. Sitting at our wooden dining table, I lifted my eyes to Andrew's and told him of the verse I had been given that morning. Andrew's eyes opened wide in surprise. He was visibly shaken. Saying nothing, he took himself off to the coolness of our shady bedroom.

A short while later, Andrew returned to the lounge and told me that he had been inwardly wrestling with the idea of taking his family to an unstable country. He didn't want to put us at risk, but the sense that God was asking us to go to South Sudan was a nagging, needling feeling that wouldn't go away. He had finally said to God that very morning that if God wanted Andrew to move there with his family, He needed to give Andrew a clear word to confirm it. The very verse I mentioned on his arrival home was so pertinent that He knew God had heard and answered.

Now Andrew was also moving closer towards saying 'yes'. Like me, he was hearing loud and clear a promise from the Lord to keep us safe. Little could we imagine, in the peace and calm of sleepy Dodoma, how very true this promise would prove to be in times of turmoil yet to come.

A strange sense of anticipation started to mix with the trepidation. I was still nervous, but God was once again developing more of my trust muscles in His spiritual gym. Out on a walk with my dependable friend Margaret a few days later, I was to be given a dose of courage to strengthen those spiritual biceps.

I confided in Margaret that Andrew and I were about to agree to being sent to South Sudan. As an experienced, long-term MAF missionary, I knew that Margaret would understand our dilemma and also the building excitement of moving to a new programme. 'But Margaret,' I confessed to her, 'I am not sure that I am brave enough to cope in a country like South Sudan. What if I'm not able to manage?'

I will always remember her response as Margaret effectively laid down the gauntlet. She gave me a challenge – a challenge I continue to relish. As we walked down that sandy Dodoma road, she looked straight at me and commented, 'Liz, the question is not, "Am I brave enough?" but rather, "Is my God big enough?" If you have faith in who God is, it doesn't matter how strong you feel.'

She had given me a clear answer. Faith was what was needed – not bravery. Could I trust in who God was? He had promised us safety. It was time to believe Him. It was time to go forward trusting that God really is 'big enough'.

20

First impressions of South Sudan

We switched off Skype, turned away from the brightly flickering computer screen and looked at each other. This was it! Andrew and I had just been speaking with the UK MAF managers to let them know that we were seriously considering South Sudan. We agreed with them that it would be a good idea to visit that programme as a family, to give us a sense of how life might be in Juba. At the end of the visit, we would give our final answer: a definitive 'yes' or 'no'. On 16 September 2013, we took a flight from Dar es Salaam, landing in Juba late afternoon.

It was the heat that I remember first. After the Kenya Airways plane came to a halt on the black tarmac of Juba airport, we shuffled our way along the busy aisle to the open door. As we reached the top of the aeroplane stairs, it felt as though we had jumped into a bath of hot water. I could almost feel the shock to my sweat glands as they prepared to be overactive. Ben looked up at me in surprise.

On the tarmac, a shimmering mirage presented a wall of heat that rose from the ground. 'I bet if we dropped an egg right here, it would be fried in no time,' I said to the children as we climbed together down the metal stairs of the plane and onto the baking apron of Juba International Airport. The sun beat down, surrounding us with intense heat. I was later to discover that intensity was a hallmark of life in this country.

Not used to the humidity, every step we took towards the immigration building felt sluggish. I was thirsty, but there was nowhere to buy a bottle of water, so we continued to make our way towards the crush of people at the visa entry point.

We entered into a small, low building where the passengers from our plane were gathered. The stale stench from the toilets located at the doorway was enough to cause our children to exclaim rudely at the overpowering odour.

Inside, we found ourselves in a large room, devoid of furniture. At one end, floor-to-ceiling, wooden booths were lined up where passports could be posted through small slots in the glass panels. Immigration officials stood behind these to process and stamp visas. The wall that ran parallel to the runway was mostly made up of a long glass window, allowing the sun to penetrate into a room already hot from sweaty bodies. There was no actual queue, but more of a disorganised push towards the booths.

Not used to elbowing our way to the front and not able to anyway with three little bodies to keep safely close to us, Andrew and I found ourselves increasingly at the back of the surge towards the immigration desks. The children grew restless as the room began to feel sweltering. Eventually, I took the children towards the window and we sat down on the dirty floor tiles. Here, we waited our turn to be granted entry into the world's newest nation.

I was suddenly struck by two observations. Firstly, most of the passengers were men and the majority of them were African. Secondly, there were no other children. I felt so obviously different. I began to notice how much we were being stared at.

'Mummy, I'm thirsty,' a little voice piped up.

'So am I,' I responded, 'but we will just have to wait until we are through that barrier to get some water.' I gestured to the rope slung across the doorway out of the room. A tall soldier with an enormous gun guarded this exit.

When our time to be stamped in finally came, I brought the children to where Andrew was standing. In front of us were two MSF (Médecins Sans Frontières) passengers, one Belgian, one Congolese. They looked at us and smiled. 'We can't believe you're bringing children into South Sudan!' they exclaimed. 'We've never seen foreigners bring children here. Did you know that many South Sudanese have their children attending schools in Kenya or Uganda?'

I laughed, but their words were disconcerting. Would my children be happy in a place with few playmates? And what were we going to do about schooling? The next few days would give us an idea of the answers.

A short while later, the five of us entered South Sudan, our passports declaring us as visitors. Bastiaan, the MAF programme manager, smiling welcomingly across the arrivals area was a happy sight. He drove us to the spacious MAF compound where, inside large, metal gates, ten homes were set loosely around a grassy, shaded plot. We were generously offered use of the home of MAF pilot family Kristen and Ryan Unger, as they were away on a short break. Their lovely home was a newly built duplex with modern furniture.

That evening, we were given a delicious dinner by kind neighbours, but it was interrupted when Ben began to cry pitifully. It was unusual for five-year-old Ben to complain, but he was fussing noisily about earache, which it seemed the flight had exacerbated. We got ready for our first night in South Sudan, putting Joel and Esther to bed but sitting up with Ben until 10 p.m., when he finally fell into an exhausted sleep from all his crying.

That first night was miserable. I woke up sweating, slipping off the sheets – we were simply not accustomed to feeling this warm. I was also aware of a loud noise – Ben, screaming. Not just crying, but really screaming. 'My ears! My ears!' Ben shouted. Tears were streaming down his chubby little cheeks.

Since he was inconsolable, I decided to bring him to our bed. We were three hot bodies on a double bed. It was hard to rest again.

As I was trying to get comfortable, I was jerked awake by the startling sound of a gunshot. I sat bolt upright in fear. Andrew leapt out of our crowded bed and rushed to the window. There was nothing to see – no sign of people, no movement outside. We discussed what to do in whispers and waited a while. When nothing more happened, we decided to settle back on the bed to get a little more slumber.

I was tense and uncertain, but tried to relax. I was almost drifting off when I became aware of more crying. Was Ben still in pain? No, this time, Joel had woken and was crying in confusion in an unfamiliar bed. Since he was equally inconsolable, I gave into his cries and brought him to our bed. Now we were four hot bodies on a double bed. Sleep was impossible.

I got up and went to look for water. I was thirsty, so thirsty. I felt like I had been thirsty since we arrived in Juba. In the dark and in this unknown house, I didn't know where to find drinking water or cups. I groped my way down to the single room where Esther was sleeping. Maybe she would have water next to her bed? But there was nothing to drink on her bedside table. I should have planned ahead and located the drinking water before we went to bed. I made my way back to our room. This time, I climbed, exhausted, into Ben's empty bed. There was more space here! I spent the next few hours restlessly tossing and turning.

When morning finally dawned, it was a relief. I wandered down to the kitchen and, spotting the water filer on the kitchen counter, quickly topped it up with jugs of tap water, then turned on its tap to fill a glass with water. Finally, I could quench my thirst, but now felt ready for a cup of tea. Opening and shutting cupboards in vain, I couldn't find a single teabag, only coffee, but it was tea I was craving. Next, I looked for milk for the children to have some cereal. There was a box of Weetabix, but no milk in the fridge. Instead, I found a large tin of powdered milk that needed to be mixed with water. This was rather different from the fresh cow's milk we boiled up in Dodoma. There was much I needed to learn about domestic life in Juba.

Without warning, I was abruptly stopped in my hunt around the kitchen as a sharp pain ripped across my stomach. A wave of nausea swept over me. I hurried to the bathroom. Feeling suddenly weak, I lowered myself tentatively on to the shiny bathroom floor as the second wave of nausea hit. The pain in my stomach jabbed my insides like a knife and I curled up in a ball as my body broke out in a clammy sweat. Blacking out, the sounds of my family getting up became distorted and distant. I lay my head on the tiles, finding solace on their solid, cold form.

Thankfully, there was a bucket within arm's reach. Once the blackness had passed, I grabbed the bucket and crawled back to the bedroom, heaving myself up on to Ben's bed and calling for Andrew. I positioned the bucket strategically by the head of the bed, within easy reach in case I needed to be sick. I started to become aware of Ben's short little legs coming closer. He padded up to my bedside, looked into the bucket by my head – and promptly vomited three times!

I couldn't bear to watch and turned my head away, feeling terrible that I was not even strong enough to help my young son. Poor Ben! It was an upsetting start to our first day in the city of our potential new home. Surely this did not bode well for the future?

Things started to turn around, though. I always think if something starts badly, it can only get better. Andrew was wonderful. He sorted out Ben, got rid of the offending bucket, gave me painkillers, changed Joel's filthy nappy, managed to mix up milk powder and fed our children bowls of Weetabix. He was Superman!

I drifted off to sleep. When I woke from a heavy morning sleep, Andrew had happily sourced teabags from a neighbour and presented me with a hot cup of tea. Despite the warmth of the morning, I was grateful for the comforting drink and started to feel better. I wasn't completely sure why I had felt unwell, but it seemed likely that it was dehydration from the previous day and night which had built up to unhealthy levels. Ben, too, had made a remarkable recovery. His unexpected, not-so-charming offering into the bucket seemed to have cured his earache.

That same morning, we had a tour of the offices on the compound, situated by the car park where we had entered yesterday. On the way round, Bastiaan reassured us that the gunshot we heard in the night was just an accidental firing of weapons and not a threat. That was good to know. The staff team in the offices and around the compound gave us a warm welcome, shaking our hands enthusiastically and smiling indulgently at the children.

The international MAF team were kind and helpful over the next few days, showing us Juba's shops and restaurants, and hosting us in their homes. Andrew and I were pleasantly surprised to observe how much more modern the facilities were, at least in the centre of town, compared to Dodoma. The MAF compound felt safe and boasted a playground and a small, refreshing swimming pool, like a large, round bathtub.

We met neighbours from World Relief, the Christian NGO who shared the compound, and were delighted to discover a South African family with two young girls who could be younger playmates for our children.

Bastiaan organised a tour of a local primary school for us. It was fascinating to look around. The teachers were welcoming and keen to answer questions. However, it was apparent that the learning system was intrinsically different from the one our children were used to in Dodoma. I was also reluctant to go along with the school motto: raising leaders in the footsteps of John Garang, the revered military leader who helped establish South Sudan's independence and after whom the school was named.

It sounded so political. We decided that homeschooling would be a better option for us, so I mentally started to prepare myself for this rather daunting role.

In the mornings, I made sure I spent time talking to the Lord about whether Juba was the place where He wanted us to come. I told Him my concerns and asked Him for answers. I should not have been surprised when He answered, but I was! The Bible verses that were part of my daily readings during our stay in Juba could not have been more apt.

Firstly, I prayed about my concerns about safety. Waking up in the night to a gunshot had enhanced my fear of the country's volatile security situation, even though the shooting we heard had not posed any danger. I raised my eyebrows in surprise when, turning to the reading outlined in my daily 'Thought for the Day', the verse was: 'Don't let your hearts be troubled. Trust in God, and trust also in me' (John 14:1, NLT).

The fact that there would be few playmates for my children was my second concern. There were a handful of children we had met or knew about, but they were much younger than Esther. Would she be happy without any peers? 'Lord, there are so few children – how will we find friends for them?' I argued. Again, the reply from my Bible reading reassured me: 'I know that you can do all things; no purpose of yours can be thwarted' (Job 42:2). If God can do 'all things', I reasoned, He can send playmates to Juba for my three children. He can likewise provide opportunities for them to thrive.

In regards to my questions about whether we would be doing the right thing by moving to Juba, I read, 'He is the Rock, his works are perfect, and all his ways are just. A faithful God who does no wrong, upright and just is he' (Deuteronomy 32:4). If he 'does no wrong', then he does not make mistakes. Therefore, I could trust his faithful nature and follow His lead to South Sudan, despite my misgivings about homeschooling and the other unknowns of life in a new country.

In short, I felt reassured on every count. By the time we climbed aboard the commercial jet for our return flight to Tanzania, we were certain of our answer. We contacted MAF and said 'YES' to South Sudan.

Back in Dodoma, preparations began in earnest for our move. Several weeks after our visit to Juba, I stood in our lounge, surrounded by the chaos of cardboard boxes, packing tape and labels. Two-year-old Joel toddled about the empty room, confused by how bare our home was. Our goods were about to go into storage until we could organise transport to South Sudan. Only essential items remained, which would be packed in our suitcases.

Our children were mentally preparing to say goodbye to their friends, school and Tanzanian life. Emotions ran high. A new MAF family from Finland had arrived in Dodoma and were waiting in a nearby guest house to move into what was almost our 'old' home. We were about to move to South Sudan!

Or so we thought.

On 15 December 2013, the BBC headlines broadcast disturbing news. South Sudan had descended into bloody fighting. Tribal tensions had boiled over, mayhem reigned in the capital city Juba and neighbours were killing neighbours. Over the following days, tales of gunfire made my blood run cold and our prayers for the people of this nation intensify. With the evacuation of the Juba MAF team to Nairobi, our plans of moving to South Sudan were suddenly jeopardised. Burning tears spilled on to my cheeks for the people caught in the conflict – and for my family. The warm Tanzanian day seemed suddenly oppressive.

'Andrew, what are we going to do now?' I blurted out.

There was no longer a place for us in Tanzania. There was no safe place for us in South Sudan. I was going to need a lot more trust as I surveyed our almost empty home and listened to silence. My question hung, unanswered, in the dusty, Dodoma air.

21

An emotional farewell

It was a strange Christmas. Our house was an empty shell as we were all packed up, but we didn't know where we were going next. Nevertheless, we celebrated with our lovely Australian MAF neighbours and with my brother, Ian. It was his first Tanzanian visit and his first Christmas barbeque.

Two days after Christmas, we hit the long roads of East Africa to drive to Nairobi and join Renew, an international conference for Christian workers. Esther excitedly pointed out the majestic, snow-capped Kilimanjaro mountain as we drew closer to the border with Kenya. We spent a fun few days at the beautiful Brackenhurst conference centre, nestled among the emerald hills of tea-farming country. But when we met new people who asked where we lived, I didn't know what to reply. Tanzania would not be home for much longer, but our future home was still unknown.

On our return to Dodoma, though, the computer on Andrew's desk blipped into life as a Skype call came in from the MAF office in the UK. Andrew calmly answered, belying our feelings of uncertainty. We were informed that there was a temporary place for us in the MAF programme in Kenya's capital city, Nairobi.

We celebrated Esther's eighth birthday with her friends, conscious that this would be the last of our family celebrations in Dodoma. It was bittersweet to see Esther happily playing with friends who she would be unlikely to see again once we moved. This is just the reality when you move countries. Then, as soon as we had picked up the wrapping paper and party leftovers, we started the countdown for our final few days in Dodoma. Less than a week later, we were on a MAF flight heading to Nairobi – not really knowing what life in Kenya would look like. Everything was suddenly happening very fast.

I will never forget waiting for that final flight out of Dodoma. Our friends and teammates gathered at the tiny airport to wave us off, where four years ago we had landed to begin our first MAF placement. Now we stood waiting for a different MAF plane to emerge out of the flawless blue sky to carry us away. A subdued group, we stood on the veranda outside the airport's small departure lounge. Swiss, New Zealander, Australian, British and Tanzanian friends were giving us encouragement as we prepared to step into the unknown.

The sun shone bright in the afternoon sky, but my heart could not reflect its brightness. There is a dullness that takes hold in the stressful hours of final departures. I was already reeling from the painful wrench of saying goodbye to Mama Kambenga. Shortly before we left our home, she had swept in with a wide piece of cotton material, a typical Tanzanian *kanga*, draped over her shoulder. The *kanga*, as colourful as her personality, was emblazoned with sunny yellows and deep blues. A profound Swahili proverb was printed across the bottom of the fabric. We both fought, unsuccessfully, to hold back the tears as we consoled each other. Our friendship had been one of my most wonderful Tanzanian blessings. We had no idea if we would ever meet again.

Andrew stood by awkwardly, but suddenly Mama Kambenga threw an arm around each of us and encircled us inside the *kanga* she had now unfolded. The three of us stood wrapped up together in a kind of homemade tent. In passionate Swahili, my dear friend prayed blessings over us – it was deeply moving. We then prayed for her and her ministry – but in English. This was no time to try and speak a foreign language. I was overwhelmed by the sense of separation working its way into my heart. When she left, our empty lounge, stripped of its furniture, echoed the hollow emptiness I felt.

Now, standing with other Dodoma friends, I felt suppressed – like a large hand was squeezing me devoid of emotion so that I could function. I dread those strange, final moments before significant departures – where there is nothing left to say, but it feels like there ought to be lots to express. Tension took root. I was caught between wanting to hold on to every moment with these special friends who had shared our Dodoma life and wanting the pain of farewell to be over.

Esther and Ben ventured out on to the warm tarmac of this quiet airport with their friends, sitting and chatting one final time. The blond and dark heads of small chums bent together as they did their last search for interesting insects or stones among the gravel at the edge of the runway.

An unsettled Joel tugged at my trouser legs. Sensitive at just two years old, he was aware of the churning waves of change. Even his toddler friends came to wave him off. It broke my heart as I anticipated the grief my children would feel once they were wrenched from their playmates.

Suddenly, the cry went up from the children, 'The plane is coming!' The adults were spurred into action, hurriedly calling the children off the empty runway and back to the safety of the veranda.

A tiny black dot appeared, so high it was like a bird with wings spread wide. It descended ever closer and finally merged into an aeroplane shape. So this was it – our transport to the next chapter.

Our friends gathered around us one last time, embracing us in a loving circle of prayer, committing us and our future to God. This gave me strength. We untangled ourselves from those final hugs and tripped over each other as I grabbed our luggage. I tried to ensure we had each bag – and all three children.

'Let's have one last photo with the Parkers!' someone shouted. There were a few chaotic minutes of calling everyone into the shot, then the photographer snapped the button and our last moments together were captured. How hard it was to smile when grief was taking hold. My mouth refused to form a smile and my eyes were shiny with unshed tears. I tried hard not to cry. Not yet. I wanted to get the children into the plane without upsetting them.

My children were clutching their teddies, needing security in something familiar as their world began to change. Somehow we climbed into the plane and I helped Esther and Ben find their seats and tighten their seatbelts while Andrew attended to Joel.

Finally strapped in, we gestured our last goodbyes through the thick glass of the window. My tears began to spill. The plane ascended slowly, revealing the Tanzanian staff standing as a crowd at the open doors of the MAF hangar, waving up at us. The tears began to overflow. Next, we spied our much-loved home, its red roof and white walls standing out against the unusual greenery of Dodoma's rainy season. Now I needed tissues. The only one of us not shedding a tear appeared to be Joel – too young to comprehend the finality of these farewells. Esther and I cried most of the way to Nairobi, Esther squeezing her teddy tight. These stuffed bears, though not real, were to offer very real comfort to my children in the rocky transition ahead.

Part Four

Kenya

JANUARY – JULY 2014

22
A tale of two cities

I didn't expect culture shock in Nairobi, yet that is what I was experiencing as I stood, rooted to the spot, adrift amid a sea of ice-cream cartons. Here in Nairobi's Nakumatt supermarket, row upon row of shiny chest freezers offered ice creams in a dizzying array of flavours. Small tubs, large tubs, ice lollies, frozen bars of Mars or Snickers ice cream: I felt utterly overwhelmed by the choice. I was like a child awed by sparkling goodies in a huge sweet shop.

Nairobi was striking – a modern marvel. After living in Dodoma, I simply couldn't believe my eyes. How could this still be East Africa?

In Dodoma, only two small cafés on dusty side streets offered us ice cream. It came in a limited variety of sizes, was nearly always the same brand (Azam) and was only available at certain times. I would drive down the bumpy road, avoiding the potholes as best I could, and enter the small ice-cream shop, grandly named the 'ice-cream parlour'. Enquiring whether I could buy a tub of ice cream today, I was told time and again that the ice cream may arrive *'kesho'* (tomorrow) or perhaps *'kesho kutwa'* (the day after tomorrow). When I eventually hit upon a day when ice cream was freshly in stock, there was no guarantee that I could get the flavour I wanted. What a contrast to westernised Nairobi.

It wasn't just the huge shopping malls, the massive selection of supermarkets nor the amount of food choice that shocked me. Heavy, chaotic traffic fought and groaned its way down Nairobi's tarred streets. There was the sheer number of people bustling about, living in a place with pavements and traffic lights. I discovered that Kenyans spoke a different kind of Swahili, mixed with English – but most Kenyans I spoke with had flawless English. Suddenly I felt robbed of the huge effort I had invested to learn Swahili in Tanzania. Our Dodoma life seemed a million miles away from this fast-moving, noisy Kenyan metropolis – and yet we had only moved across the border. How could the country next door be so different?

Even my clothes felt strangely inappropriate. Dodoma had demanded, out of courtesy for local sensitivities, conservative clothing: long skirts to cover our legs and shirts which hid our shoulders. Jeans were frowned upon, since they showed too much of the leg's shape – though Dodoma was too hot to wear jeans anyway. In Dodoma, our clothes were often locally made from fabrics we chose at the market or from shops selling roll after roll of colourful, printed material. Our latest outfit was measured, cut and created by a seamstress sitting at her sewing machine on the side of the road. We wore heavy sandals, practical for the uneven, dusty surfaces we traipsed over in Dodoma's market and along the unpaved roads. In Nairobi, these same clothes and shoes felt ungainly, unattractive. I began to notice how faded our clothes were after drying them outside in the unrelenting sunlight of Dodoma. I felt out of place and unfashionable.

When I saw MAF ladies and the mums at our children's new school comfortably wearing Western-style clothing – showing their shoulders, with shorts or skirts above the knee – I was taken aback. I had clearly become more immersed in conservative Tanzanian culture than I realised. I was struggling to adjust my cultural expectations. I was surprised by Nairobi's shops offering expensive clothes with brand names I recognised from South Africa or England. There was such a striking contrast between my Dodoma world and the world in which I was now living.

Nairobi's cold, rainy mornings and chilly evenings were also a world away from our Tanzanian experience. This was a very different kind of Africa – and it was a difference for which we had not had time to prepare. I didn't understand this place and we didn't fit in. I questioned God, 'Why have you brought us here, Lord?'

Unlike the reassurances and clear answers I heard from Him in Juba, I now heard nothing. Just silence.

23

An unexpected kindness

'Mum, please can you feed Teddy at lunchtime?' Esther pleaded, tears welling up in her blue eyes. A new day meant Esther once again had to enter a classroom full of strangers. Her fear was reflected in her young face. She so badly wanted to take her friend – her trusted Teddy – to school and hated leaving 'her' at home.

I promised to do so, but still had to wrestle Teddy out of Esther's tight, hugging arms. She kept protesting even as I took the soft, brown bear and strapped 'her' into a seatbelt in the back of our car. Ben followed Esther's lead and solemnly handed over his green, fluffy teddy.

At lunchtime, Joel helped me set the two teddies at the dining table. We placed a plate of snacks in front of each teddy and took a photo to show Esther and Ben when they returned home from their new school in Nairobi. It had been a shock for them to suddenly start there less than a week after arriving in the country. In hindsight, if I had to make such a move again, I would have levered my children in more gently.

Every day, Esther dressed Teddy. At night, she slept with Teddy nestled in her arms. When we referred to 'Teddy' as a toy or as 'it', Esther became upset. 'Teddy is a girl!' she insisted.

Before our move from Dodoma, Esther never took much notice of soft toys, but suddenly Teddy represented a link with a world she had lost and to which she could not get back. If Esther knew Mum was looking after Teddy, part of her world from 'before' was safe. She missed her friends; she missed her teacher; she missed all that was secure, comfortable and pastoral about her Dodoma school.

For the children, life couldn't be more different. From a small, mostly Tanzanian school in quieter Dodoma, Esther and Ben were catapulted into big-city Braeburn School. Class sizes overawed them, and they felt like faceless students instead of cared-for individuals. To say Esther disliked her new school would be an understatement.

In Tanzania, Esther had easily been top of the class simply by virtue of having English as her first language. In Nairobi, the competition was much tougher. There were more students with English as a first language and students with high-flying parents who pushed their children harder. Academic expectations were higher and the workload heavier. It was a shock for Esther to discover that she was no longer one of the top students. Just a couple of weeks after turning eight, she was old enough to resist change with all that she could muster, but too young to do this in a self-controlled way.

My little girl was transformed into a different person. Sunny and bright, helpful and full of energy in Tanzania, she was now angry, frustrated and uncooperative. On school mornings, she hid under the bed, or in the bath, or behind the small, uncomfortable sofa in our temporary house. She yelled when I tried to coax her into the car for another school day.

As the car drew closer to the gates of Braeburn School, Esther's tears would start. 'I'm *NOT* going to that school!' she announced. 'I don't like it and I don't have any friends. Everyone is nasty here! I want to be back in Miss Presley's class and I wish I could play with Seche and Grace and Snigdha.' Esther was constantly referring to the friends and teacher she missed from Dodoma.

Ben in turn started to cry, frightened by his sister's anxieties and becoming worried himself.

When we finally reached Braeburn, Esther ran away from her classroom more than once. One morning, she hid among the vehicles in the car park and had to be dragged into class under my left arm while I dangled two-year-old Joel under my right arm. It was upsetting for her, for me, for her younger brothers and for her new teacher.

My children's world had changed too fast. They sorely missed their house, their playmates, their cat, all that they understood as 'home'. Their expectation had been to move to Juba, a place we had visited together as a family, where homeschool would be a safe option with Mum as their teacher. Instead, we found ourselves in a giant city, surrounded by people confident in their own lives. We were suddenly an inconvenience – short-term people who disrupted the ordered lives of others. In addition, we were short-termers who didn't want to be there – and who didn't know how long we were staying.

Was it worth putting in the effort to get to know people? From the perspective of Nairobi dwellers, were we worth investing in? They had busy schedules and found it hard to meet up with friends they already knew, never mind trying to find time for people passing through.

As my children struggled, so did I. After battling Esther into her classroom and reassuring Ben, I strapped Joel into his car seat and braced myself to fight my way back home through the Nairobi traffic. Popping a CD of lively worship music into the car's music player, I wove through cars and *matatus* (minibus taxis). I tried to join in with the upbeat singing, but instead found myself grieving for Dodoma, tears streaming down my face. I was ashamed of how I must have looked to other motorists. My roots in Tanzania had gone deeper than I thought. I was desperately missing my own friends while grieving my children's losses too.

But God is kind. My mum once told me that God sees our tears and stores them up, releasing them as blessings at a later time. I was about to see Him doing this for me.

One sunny afternoon, during our early days of transition, Joel and I had just picked up Esther and Ben from school and I was gingerly driving the four of us home down Nairobi's hectic Gitanga Road. As the traffic was heavy, we were crawling along at a snail's pace and I glanced out of the car window – to my astonishment spotting an English lady I knew walking along the pavement! Susie had attended the same Renew conference at Brackenhurst as us and we swapped email addresses because our daughters had got on so well. Although we had never managed to connect, I was certain that I still had Susie's email address. It should be easy to find, scribbled somewhere in my journal.

The traffic moved on and I had no opportunity to wave to Susie, but I was excited. Here was a connection for my grieving daughter with a little girl she knew and got on well with. It was also a connection for me with a fellow Brit; there is something special about meeting up with people from one's own country in a foreign land. I knew that Susie also had a son around Ben's age and a younger daughter similar in age to Joel. While we didn't know them well, I was sure we would get along easily.

How incredible that they were here, right near the children's school, in such an enormous city. How fantastic that Susie *just happened* to be walking down the street at the very time I *just happened* to be passing by. It was too big a coincidence. This had to be a kindness from our loving Father God.

Once home, I raced upstairs to rifle through my papers and journals. Finding Susie's email address, I lost no time in emailing her. A short while later, she sent a warm, positive response. Although Susie's children attended a different school than Braeburn, their home was close to Esther and Ben's school. It wasn't long before play dates and meals with Susie's family became a regular feature of our Nairobi life. For me and Joel, it was great to have Susie and her youngest child to spend time with during the morning hours, while the older children were at school. Joel joined a gym class with Susie's youngest daughter and that helped to bring structure at a time when we felt lost. As for Esther and Ben, they now had playmates they related to easily outside of the pressures of a new school.

It was, as ever, impeccable timing. Their friendship with us and our children was perfect for this season, stamped with the hallmark of our loving Heavenly Father who works out the intricate details. He provided for us in this specific way, with a kindness that was as startling as the gift of beautiful surprises on a birthday morning. However, it was a while before I was able to see the gifts God showered us with in Nairobi. The struggle of transitioning too fast took me and Andrew through a rocky season of doubt.

24

God is seemingly silent

I was about to cross a spiritual desert, where the God I had felt so close to seemed suddenly far away, distant – and silent.

To be honest, I couldn't blame God if He had gone quiet. I was acting like a spoilt child. Just as my daughter protested at having to go to a school she didn't want to be at, I protested at being in a country I didn't expect to live in. 'I wish there was a magic door I could walk through to take me out of Nairobi,' I stormed to God – and even to my husband.

I wanted to escape from a situation that I could not control. I was refusing to be patient. For both me and Andrew, it was a dark time spiritually. We could not understand why we had heard God speaking to us so clearly about South Sudan, only to find ourselves in Kenya. It wouldn't matter so much if the children enjoyed being in Nairobi – but they were confused and unhappy. It wouldn't matter so much if we had a fixed time frame – but we weren't sure how much time we had here. I didn't want to pour my energy into settling down, only to move again. The MAF plane had flown us from familiar Dodoma and deposited us on to the hard tarmac of a city we didn't know or understand. The sudden transition to Nairobi didn't make sense after all our mental and practical preparations for Juba. Questions jangled in my mind, in Andrew's mind – as grating as alarm bells, but without clear answers.

'Was God just testing us, to see if we would be obedient to His call?' Andrew wondered aloud. 'Did He just want us to show Him that we would be willing to go to Juba? Maybe He never wanted us to go to South Sudan?' Andrew was quieter than before; his usual joy was dulled.

'Did we hear wrongly?' I asked, all the while feeling that this could not be so. God had always proved reliable in the past. He never tricked His people: that simply wasn't consistent with His loving character. *Maybe He didn't care, after all?* was the tempting thought that snaked its way into my mind. I worked hard to dismiss the doubts about God's character, but searching for truth about how much He cared was hard when I felt so confused. At church, tears dripped from my eyes and silence replaced praise when it was time to stand and sing. My heart was grieving Tanzania. My mind was questioning God.

The spiritual questions lined up alongside the practical questions. Would we be in Kenya for weeks, months, or longer? MAF then emailed to inform us that we could not stay in Kenya long-term. If South Sudan and Kenya were not options, should we start preparing to move somewhere else? We didn't want to finish working with MAF, but was this perhaps the end of a chapter? Should we make plans to return to England? Or was it better to wait and keep an eye on events in South Sudan, still hoping to get there? And what should we do with our household goods, which were still stored in Tanzania?

In our Nairobi house, the borrowed furniture, kitchen equipment, bedding and towels all shouted, 'Temporary!' They were constant visual reminders that we were in limbo. It is easy to look back and wonder why I got myself so worked up about a situation I could not resolve – but the uncertainty triggered in me a frustration. Time after time, I questioned God about how long this season would last. I wanted to take charge and make decisions and move things on. I hated feeling so unsettled.

Yet despite the perceived silence from God, He was still active. He started to prepare others to help me. He started to put things in place to get me ready for future challenges that lay ahead. And it all started when a neighbour turned up on my doorstep one lunchtime, taking me by surprise in more ways than one.

I was just sitting down to lunch with Joel when I heard the ring of our doorbell. Before answering the door, I secured Joel in his booster chair and pulled him slightly away from the dining table and any mischief. Last time I left him alone to go and answer a knock at the door, he had shoved a baked bean up his nostril and given us both a fright! (Thankfully, it was soft enough to be blown out easily.) Then, smoothing back my hair in readiness, I opened our wooden door – but was totally unprepared for the greeting I received.

'Liz,' my neighbour Rachel said, smiling at me. 'I've been praying for you today. The Lord told me that you are in denial about homeschooling your children.'

What? I questioned silently. I didn't quite know how to respond – but clearly the lady standing in front of me cared about me. She also knew exactly what she was talking about, having homeschooled her own three children while serving with MAF in turbulent East Timor.

'I want to help you get ready,' she proposed.

Rachel and I made a plan to brainstorm resources and curriculum ideas. She had brilliant ideas about books, toys and games to help me homeschool. She also kindly offered to scout second-hand sales so that I could stock up on resources – something she did so well that crate after crate kept appearing on my doorstep. Maybe God wasn't speaking loudly to me in this season, but He was definitely speaking to Rachel! Many months later, I was to pull those resources from the shelves of our homeschool room in Juba and thank God for the insight he gave Rachel.

Rachel was not alone in being supportive. Other MAF mums rallied round. Resourceful Lindsay rapidly sourced the uniform, sports kit and even school shoes we needed. I was grateful for her support too when she ran after my miserable children on the school campus, comforting them when I was too emotional to do so myself. Other ladies offered me their valuable time, and tea, even though I knew they had hectic schedules. Several invited us for meals. Each invitation was cherished and appreciated. I honestly don't know how we would have managed those early, tumultuous days at Braeburn School without their help.

A short while after our arrival in Nairobi, another MAF family arrived, also bound for South Sudan. Our two families waited to see what would be next, praying for peace in South Sudan. Although their baby was younger than my three children, spending time together was a comfort as we shared our common concern. Karyn and I started to take her baby and Joel to a weekly activity group, Baby Bible Class, which provided me and Joel with another friendly community in this season. Karyn also proposed that we should attempt a few Arabic lessons together, with a teacher from Juba. Unfortunately, my brain was still too full of Swahili to absorb anything of lasting value in tricky Arabic. In addition, I was distracted during the lessons by Joel's antics as he played next to me and clambered under the table.

On Friday mornings, I joined the MAF Kenya ladies for their weekly Bible study group, with Joel coming along too. Their studies focused on the Psalms of Ascent (Psalms 120–146), and I found strength in their words and honest emotions. As I read Psalm 121, I was convicted by the truth. My eyes danced over the words: 'My help comes from the LORD, the Maker of heaven and earth… the LORD will watch over your coming and going' (verses 2 and 8).

God was watching over us – whether here in Nairobi, or 'going' to South Sudan. He was helping me through this season of uncertainty and providing for our every need, despite my frustration and impatience.

Maybe God had not been silent after all. Maybe I had just been looking for the wrong kind of answers, when all that was needed was to be still – and wait for my Helper to open the way.

25

Trouble in Kenya

While we waited on God and learnt to live in Nairobi, Andrew was kept busy. It had taken longer than he expected to pass the necessary aviation exams which converted his Tanzanian flying licence to a Kenyan licence. Having been grounded until the paperwork was completed, he was relieved to be in the cockpit again. Now his work as a MAF pilot could continue and he gained more experience – with some unusual adventures along the way.

The first of these occurred while Andrew was on his first supervised flight in Kenya, with his colleague Daniel. These flights would help Andrew to get used to flying the Cessna Caravan operationally and give him exposure to this new environment while another experienced pilot was close at hand. Andrew and Daniel were headed to Marsabit, with a scheduled first stop at a tiny rocky outpost named Korr. Two people at the Catholic Mission there had requested a MAF flight. Coming down to land, Andrew took in the sparse, scorched landscape.

The plane descended gracefully and came to a stop on the airstrip at Korr. After picking up the two passengers, it took off again for the short hop to Marsabit. Ominous clouds were gathering and the skies looked less and less friendly. As the small plane approached Marsabit, the weather worsened. It became obvious that landing there would not be a possibility.

Andrew needed to make a safe decision – quickly. Without any suitable alternatives, he turned the nose of the aircraft and flew back to Korr. When the MAF plane circled over Korr airstrip and came in to land for the second time that day, the Catholic Fathers at the Don Bosco Mission were surprised – they did not expect to see them back so soon.

The stormy weather kept closing in – there was no possibility of take-off for Andrew, Daniel and their two passengers. They were stuck in the middle of nowhere – what were the four of them going to do? Thankfully, the Catholic Fathers were hospitable, inviting Andrew and Daniel to join them on the mission compound overnight while their passengers made separate arrangements.

As Andrew had not expected to be away, he did not have a pilot's usual overnight bag, with a spare uniform, pyjamas, underwear and, of course, a toothbrush. He made the best of the situation and the next day – with a crumpled shirt, dusty trousers and unbrushed teeth –

started up the MAF plane. With the propeller whirring and the engine roaring, the two pilots and their passengers once more took off for Marsabit. This time, the weather was kind and there were blue skies.

As the plane touched down in Marsabit, though, something didn't feel right. Stopping on the runway to disembark the passengers, Andrew and Daniel climbed down from the cockpit to find that the nose wheel tyre was completely flat. After discussing the problem with MAF in Nairobi, a smaller Cessna 206 was dispatched along with equipment and an engineer to make the necessary repairs.

Both pilots and passengers worked hard to roll the stricken aircraft clear of the runway in order to make space for the inbound flight. It was hot, sweaty work in this semi-arid region of northern Kenya. Andrew and Daniel were relieved when they could eventually stand in the shade of the wings to wait for assistance. The recovery team duly arrived and the engineer made the plane airworthy again.

It was a tired Andrew who eventually arrived back in Nairobi a day later than planned, happy to finally get home, shower and brush his teeth! Since that day, Andrew has never forgotten an overnight kit – just in case of unexpected delays.

Andrew's second adventure during those months in Kenya occurred one ordinary, sunny afternoon. As Andrew jumped into the car after a long day at work and pulled out of the car park at Nairobi's Wilson Airport, his mobile phone started to ring, jigging up and down as it vibrated on the dashboard. Since the car was still moving slowly and not yet on the main road, Andrew answered the call. He could see my name flashing up on the screen, so decided to quickly speak to me then hang up, before joining the traffic on Langata Road.

'Hello, darling,' he heard me say, my voice resonating through the tinny speaker of his phone.

'Hi, Liz!' Andrew sounded quite chipper as we began our conversation.

A few seconds later, Andrew's tone changed and he became distracted. 'Ehm, Liz, I need to go' he said urgently.

'Why?' I asked. There was a brief fumbling noise and Andrew muttered something vague about police officers, then the phone was cut off.

'Oh dear,' I muttered. Kenyan traffic police are known to be strict when they encounter any violation of traffic law, and it seemed that Andrew had been caught in the illegal act of speaking on a mobile phone while driving. No matter that Andrew was moving at a crawling pace – the principle was the same.

I didn't hear from Andrew for the next hour or so – and didn't dare call him again. When he finally arrived home after his encounter with the police and having then fought his way through crazy traffic, my suspicions were proved correct. My husband walked in with a bruised ego – and a summons to court for a traffic violation!

The saga ended a few days later. Andrew went to court, pleaded guilty as he rightfully should and was ordered to

WHERE IT ALL BEGAN (1967 – 2004)

Liz's Mum, Ann, with village children in Uganda.

SOUTH AFRICA & ENGLAND (NOVEMBER 2004 – NOVEMBER 2009)

Andrew trains as a Pilot at 43 Air School.

Esther and Liz enjoy the beaches of South Africa.

Welcoming Benjamin Parker.

TANZANIA (NOVEMBER 2009 - JANUARY 2014)

Andrew with former witch-doctor, Abraham, and a Maasai Evangelist.

Children gather in the shade of the MAF plane.

Mothers queue up at the monthly MAF mother and baby clinic.

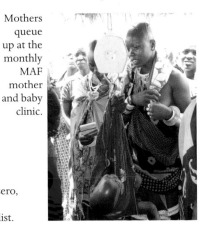

Engaresero, Maasai Evangelist.

Jane, the wonderful house-help, with baby Joel.

Avoiding an unwelcome dangerous visitor.

Iringa Language School – Kiswahili language lesson.

Market shopping in Dodoma.

Ben helps to clean meat, freshly arrived
from the market on slaughter day.

Very orange but very comfortable
– pregnant in Dodoma.

KENYA (JANUARY - JULY 2014)

Inseparable – Teddy and Esther.

Esther starts to enjoy Nairobi – At the elephant orphanage.

SOUTH SUDAN (AUGUST 2014 - JULY 2016)

Joel and Moses on the Juba doorstep.

Home-school room, Juba. (Photo credit LuAnne Cadd)

All in a day's work!
(Photo Credit LuAnne Cadd)

Andrew loading the MAF plane.
(Photo Credit LuAnne Cadd)

Delighted that Susan is standing again. Susan and Carolyn, Juba Teaching Hospital.

Andrew meets Baroness Cox in Arua.

Mud-monsters – MAF boys having fun!

Esther meets a Granny at the Christmas Parcel Distribution.

July 9th 2016 Evacuation – getting ready to depart on the MAF plane from Juba.

Flying with Dad on the way to Kenya.

Ben's picture of what he was exposed to on July 9th 2016.

NAIROBI (2016)

Safe in Kenya – Black Rose – the Parker's ground floor apartment home.

UGANDA (DECEMBER 2016 ONWARDS)

A new home in Uganda. Parker kids with friend Moses from Juba just after they arrived.

KOTIDO (AUGUST 2017)

Liz's Mum, Ann, returns to Kotido, Uganda.

Mum waves goodbye to Kotido again, 50 years after her last departure.

The Parker Family, 2014. (Photo credit LuAnne Cadd)

pay his fine – but there was a catch. Under the Kenyan system, all offenders are held in a cell with other traffic offenders until the fines are paid. Furthermore, offenders can only be released when the payment has been made at a specific local bank and the receipt returned to the officials for verification. Fortunately, Andrew had come to court accompanied by a Kenyan colleague, Mark. As Andrew was taken away to his cell, Mark rushed off to pay the required amount as quickly as possible, collected the receipt and returned it to court so that Andrew could be released.

While Mark was busy getting to and from the bank, Andrew spent two hours as a captive within the Kenyan justice system, locked up in a roomy cell with several other men who were also waiting for their traffic fines to be paid. There was plenty of time for conversation and one of Andrew's new jail comrades snapped a photo of Andrew on his phone camera. We now have living proof of Andrew's Kenyan adventure, which will forever remind him to ignore a ringing mobile phone while driving – even if his wife is calling!

Three months after arriving in Nairobi, we heard that the situation was stabilising in South Sudan. MAF families who had evacuated in December returned to their Juba homes. From April onwards, Andrew started to spend alternate weeks in Juba, flying for the South Sudan MAF programme, while the children and I stayed in Nairobi. He was learning more about flying in South Sudan – and started to look forward to our possible move to Juba in the next few months.

26

Resistance to gratitude

It was around this time that I became aware of a change. My resistance to Nairobi was thawing. My grief-stained view of Nairobi started to give way to a more positive outlook. I began to notice the blessings God was giving us. By the time we left Kenya in July 2014, Nairobi had become a city with friends and happier family memories, despite the shaky start.

A culmination of factors carried me from resistance to acceptance. It started with the visit of a MAF family based in Dodoma who had an incredibly caring heart. After dinner, they took time to ask us how things really were and how we honestly felt in this uncertain season. They listened attentively to our candid answers then prayed with and for us, reassuring us that our reaction was normal, that our concerns were heard. I sometimes wonder if they realised just how much their gift of time meant to us in that confusing season.

Perhaps the thaw began even earlier, when we determined to distract our grieving children by taking advantage of Nairobi's tourist attractions, beginning a growing appreciation for the opportunities an active city like Nairobi offered. Saturdays became days to explore. One weekend, we visited Nairobi's giraffe centre and gazed in wonder at the tall, graceful creatures. Ben tempted one of the animals closer with round pellets of grain. When the giraffe swept the tasty treats off Ben's hand and into its mouth with its dark, rolling tongue, Ben squealed with delight. Joel was more apprehensive, which was fair enough considering how giant these creatures were compared to his three-year-old frame! It was good to see Esther relax as we enjoyed the adventure of hand-feeding giraffes from a high wooden platform.

On a different Saturday morning at Nairobi's elephant orphanage, Esther, Ben and Joel yelled in excitement when a baby elephant stomped into a muddy puddle, splashing me from head to toe in red mud. I laughed with the children as we snapped a photograph of my mud-splattered outfit. After watching the elephants' feeding time, the children were intrigued to observe a football match between the calves. It was an incredible privilege to be so close to such majestic yet vulnerable animals.

Then, on the advice of other MAF families, we made the small sacrifice of getting up before dawn to visit Nairobi National Park. Our reward was a magnificent drive down meandering pathways, spotting a variety of wildlife. We felt a million miles away from the bustling city. Only the high-rise buildings shimmering in the heat on the horizon gave any hint that we were still in Kenya's metropolis. The children thrust their heads out of the car windows, competing to be the first to view a zebra, a wildebeest, a giraffe.

We also discovered the green space of Karua Forest on the edge of the city, where we moved like intrepid explorers, tramping down shady pathways under the leafy canopy. Black-and-white colobus monkeys chattered in the treetops and tiny, golden deer darted through the undergrowth. It was refreshing to have these windows into nature despite the heaving bustle of traffic-filled streets so close by. The forest became a regular outing – a place our children looked forward to visiting and a space to run off energy. We gradually noticed our daughter returning to her usual, sunny self.

One of the special blessings of those months in Nairobi was our proximity to Andrew's sister, Claire. After living so close to us in Dodoma for two of our four years there, she had since moved to Kenya and worked as a teacher at St Andrew's School, Turi. Although Turi was a four-hour drive from Nairobi, Claire spent several weekends with us. The children were soothed by the presence of their auntie – a much-loved, familiar friend in this season of new faces. One of Claire's visits was spent chasing and catching a bold and rude rat in our house after it ate its way through our food, but there were far more exciting moments as we helped Claire plan for her upcoming wedding. A highlight of my time in Kenya was helping Claire find her beautiful wedding gown in a shop at Nairobi's Yaya Shopping Centre.

After a few months, I realised that my grief for our Tanzanian life was easing, allowing thankfulness for all we had in this new season. Kenya was starting to push roots into my heart, these tender, green shoots intertwining with my more established Tanzania roots. I was learning to appreciate variety in our East African experiences.

By the beginning of July, we heard that Juba had remained calm and that the work for MAF pilots in South Sudan was plentiful. It was finally time to move there and we were excited about what lay ahead. I packed up our temporary Nairobi home, with its new memories of God's grace to us. When the time came to say 'goodbye' to Nairobi, I had come to value the gifts God provided for us in this city.

I looked forward to unpacking our own household goods in South Sudan. They had arrived in Nairobi from Tanzania and were being prepared for transportation to Juba by MAF plane. It would be good to unpack in a house we could call 'home' rather than simply a stopgap one. I was also excited about arranging the homeschool materials which Rachel had helped me stock, as well as our shiny, brand-new, homeschool curriculum which had arrived at Kenyan customs from England's Worldwide Education Service.

Esther and Ben ended on a good note at Braeburn School after two terms there. Despite the challenging transition, Braeburn School had been good for them. They had been stretched academically, giving me a better idea of what they could achieve. I left Nairobi with clearer academic expectations as I prepared to incorporate 'teacher' as well as 'mum' to my domestic job title. Rachel was right – I had been unprepared for homeschooling when we first arrived in Nairobi, but these six months had allowed me time to better prepare for this new role.

God knew I needed a stepping stone to Juba – so He gave me Nairobi. I was ashamed that I had doubted His goodness, but grateful that my resistance did not prevent His plans.

When we said goodbye to our new friends in Nairobi, our farewells felt light. In a big city, lives are naturally lived more separately, so we had not bonded with friends the way we did in Dodoma's tight-knit environment. We also knew that we would be passing though Nairobi every three months, for a week or two at a time. This was part of the R and R (Rest and Recreation) cycle given to MAF staff working in politically volatile environments like Juba. Dodoma goodbyes had left a sad question hanging in the air: 'Will we ever meet again?' The Nairobi goodbyes were easier: they held the promise of reunion. We left Nairobi with a smile, not tears.

As I reflected on these six months, I felt thankful for the faithfulness of a God who was silently working out the details of our Nairobi life. Unbeknown to us, these six months were to be the basis for another period when we would find ourselves unexpectedly returning to live in Kenya. Thankfully, God already knew that and had graciously given us a foundation in this African city.

Part Five

South Sudan

AUGUST 2014 - JULY 2016

27

South Sudan - at last!

Sweat was dripping down my neck and down my back. My hair felt moist and I just knew I had an unattractive moisture moustache forming on my top lip! However, I resolutely refused to be outdone by the heat. Stubbornly keeping to my British roots, I sipped a hot mug of tea, carefully holding a slice of birthday cake in my other hand. It was the day of my fortieth birthday – and the day after we arrived in Juba. If life begins at forty, then I was at the brink of my new life in this new country. I was feeling reassured by the warm welcome we had received as we joined our teammates for an impromptu afternoon birthday tea.

Here we were, at last, in South Sudan: the world's newest nation. This land of intense heat. A country whose people had learnt resilience the hard way, with its chequered history of war and heartbreak. A people who took pride in their new flag and their newly gained independence.

The relentless sun bore down, but the greenery surrounding our MAF compound offered some shade. The sounds of city life, of traffic and construction sites, of people moving and of street vendors and buyers were muted but still evident. While Juba was South Sudan's capital city, the MAF compound, where offices and house converged, was a safe, sheltered space. It was situated in Juba's Hai Cinema district, a thriving hub of local businesses, hotels and NGO offices. New development contrasted with the rough, basic houses that mostly lined the streets. The district was built on the hope that South Sudan would move forward to stability and peace.

Two delicious cakes sat out on plates, covered from the incessant flies which buzzed about in the heat. I was touched by the kindness of two of our MAF neighbours who had gone to the effort of baking for my birthday. This kind gesture had been organised by my thoughtful husband, since he knew how much birthdays mean to me. He didn't want this one to go uncelebrated because of the hectic activity of moving countries. Two wooden picnic tables situated by the small, raised swimming pool made this central area a natural gathering place. It was a great way to start meeting our new colleagues. Nearby, the children were playing on the metal climbing frame or bouncing on the trampoline, which was sensibly set up in the shade.

'Mum! Look at me!' An upside-down Ben hung from the bars of the climbing frame, having the time of his life and waving his loose arms to get my attention. Ben was already striking up a comradery with Caleb, whose house we had stayed in during our 2013 visit. I looked for Joel and noticed that he was shyly playing alongside neighbour Moses, who was just a year older than him. Then I spotted Esther climbing up to the top of the metal slide with Emma, our new Dutch neighbour. Although Emma was four years younger than Esther, theirs was to be a loyal friendship. I waved back at Ben and inwardly marvelled that God was already starting to answer my prayers for playmates. A year earlier, when we had first visited Juba, I had come to the Lord fretful and concerned about the lack of other children for Esther, Ben and Joel to socialise with – but God had gone ahead of us, already lining up friends.

Teatime finished. The children and I walked the short distance across the compound, past the enormous, black tanks where trucks came to fill up our water supply, past the car park and the prefabricated office buildings and along a short, concrete path to our house. We climbed the steep front doorstep and pushed the heavy, glass front door to enter our new spacious and modern home. There, we hung curtains, arranged cupboards and settled in. Unpacking in our new house was fun – as we tore lids off boxes, we found items we hadn't seen for eight months. We loved the excitement of rediscovering toys, books and household goods. It was as though we each had gifts to open on my birthday! Esther and Ben were also thrilled with the handsome, grey cat we inherited from the previous occupants of our MAF home.

I was a little less thrilled to discover in the kitchen one afternoon that we had also inherited a colony of cockroaches! I screamed in horror as I pulled out a kitchen drawer to find no less than thirty – yes, *thirty* – of these nasty creepy-crawlies. They scuttled this way and that over the kitchen tiles, taunting me with their boldness, waving their antennae as if to goad me. I uncovered my darker side as I energetically sprayed poison on my small but numerous enemies.

Andrew was busy flying for MAF within days of our arrival in Juba. Since he had spent time flying in South Sudan during the previous months, he was already familiar with the routine. Andrew loved the work, loved the flying, loved the interaction with the team. He felt privileged to be part of such a busy programme and could see first-hand the positive impact the MAF flights had in bringing aid and hope to the people of this war-torn nation. Most of his work required flying in-country, meaning that he was rarely away overnight. It was good to know he would be mostly based at home – a nice contrast for us after his frequent overnight absences from Nairobi and Dodoma.

28

Learning to homeschool

Some people are natural homeschoolers. I am not one of them!

After my years of being a primary school teacher, I thought I knew how to teach. I had set up our homeschool room, thanks to our time in Nairobi and thanks to Rachel, and felt prepared. I therefore thought that it would be easy to homeschool. So why was I standing in the middle of our homeschool room feeling ready to explode?

It was like a scene from a television comedy, except that this was our reality. Esther, still eight, was in tears. Ben was huffing and puffing, his arms folded rebelliously across his six-year-old chest. Three-year-old Joel was lying on the floor, shouting and banging a fistful of crayons against the white tiles. I kept asking myself why teaching a class of thirty children belonging to other adults was so much easier than teaching my own children. What would our

MAF supporters say if they could see the chaotic real-life scene of this family whose work they helped to support?

'If you loved me, you wouldn't give me such hard maths to do!' Esther declared, glaring accusingly at me.

I was indignant. 'Esther!' I exclaimed, 'This has absolutely NOTHING to do with love. This maths exercise is EXACTLY the same as what all other Year Four students will be doing all over England because this is the curriculum. This is NOT something I made up just to make your life difficult!'

My daughter eyed me suspiciously, but I was determined to win this battle.

Meanwhile, Ben was resisting his writing task. My fiery side was still sparking. 'Ben, you can't just sit there doing nothing – pick up your pencil and practise your words.'

'I don't like writing!' he retorted.

'It's not about liking something, it's about practising to get better at something – in this case, learning to use those words on the list in front of you.'

On Ben's list was the word 'were'. Eventually, Ben bent to his writing, but I could see that his rebellion was still festering.

A few minutes later, Ben shoved his paper across the desk towards me. 'I wrote this for you,' he said, gruffly.

I looked at the page and had to hide a smile as I read his somewhat apt sentence: 'Were you kind?'

There was a reminder for me there. Homeschooling was as much about my character development as it was about the children's education. Time after time, I came across Bible verses which convicted me. I called them my 'homeschooler' verses. I had to return to them constantly to pray them in, asking God for more grace to put them into practice. Often, the first words out of my mouth showed frustration – but God was using this homeschooling to grow and challenge me.

My homeschooling verses were:

- 'A gentle answer turns away wrath, but a harsh word stirs up anger' (Proverbs 15:1)

- '... gracious words promote instruction' (Proverbs 16:21)

- 'The hearts of the wise [of teachers!] make their mouths prudent, and their lips promote instruction' (Proverbs 16:23)

- 'Gracious words are a honeycomb, sweet to the soul' (Proverbs 16:24)

It took several months before we got into a rhythm with homeschooling. One massive change which made it much easier was the incredibly generous gift of a prefabricated learning room from the mission support group at St Michael's Church in London. When it arrived on the back of a truck, it caused great excitement. The children were fascinated as it was efficiently erected a few metres away from our house. I enjoyed setting it up as a classroom with colourful posters, desks, chairs and bookcases. We displayed the children's work on the thin, metal walls using magnets – the easiest display solution I have ever come across.

What a relief to have a schoolroom that was no longer in the house. Apart from the extra space, it allowed me two gifts. The first was interacting with other adults. I now had to actually go out of the house and across the compound to reach the schoolroom. As I walked over, I greeted the South Sudanese staff who worked in MAF's facilities section by the office complex. It was refreshing to have adult conversations as part of my daytime routine. I felt part of the wider world again, rather than shut off in the house all day.

The second, even more significant gift was the psychological benefit of separating 'school' from 'home'. When school was set up in our front room, I found it a strain to be simultaneously working with the children and surrounded by domestic chores. As soon as I finished fractions with Esther, I would glance up and spy the laundry waiting impatiently to be hung outdoors. A few steps away, piles of dirty dishes sat reproachfully in the kitchen sink, itching to be washed. It felt like my work never ended. Once we moved out of the house, I could ignore domestic tasks and focus on schoolwork without that extra tension.

Help also came in the form of cheerful, bustling Grace Sunday. This tall, well-built South Sudanese lady, with her dark hair tightly braided and wearing a long, brown skirt and T-shirt, came to my rescue two and a half days every week. I was grateful for her jolly disposition as her huge smile greeted me in the morning. Grace went to work with gusto, sorting out those dirty dishes and arranging the laundry on the line outside. Armed with her mop, she attacked filthy marks on the floor tiles and left them sparkling. Beads of sweat on her forehead bore testament to her hard work in this hot climate.

Once we moved into the school room outside, I loved popping home during lesson breaks on Grace's work days and finding our home neat and organised. I grabbed a *clean* mug – hooray! – and made myself a quick cup of tea, breathing a huge sigh of thankfulness for Grace Sunday.

For Joel, schooling was a different matter. As Esther and Ben started work at their desks at 8.30, I walked Joel to the new preschool across the other side of our compound. With only five students – from five different nations – and two teachers, JCA (Juba Christian Academy) was just getting underway. It was a beautifully caring and nurturing environment for little ones. In the early days, Joel went to school until 12 p.m. He was mostly happy, though shy and missed his siblings.

After lunch, Joel joined us for the afternoons. However, having a preschooler in the classroom could be tricky. The WES (Worldwide Education Service) homeschool schedule was fast-paced and demanding. I had to email schoolwork samples to tutors in the UK every four weeks, so I was keen to keep the learning up to date. This necessity often clashed with Joel's needs and created conflict. Joel was so young, yet his mum was so distracted by schoolwork. He resisted activities I tried to engage him in, partly because he was tired after his active morning and simply wanted to play with his siblings. For the first year in Juba, trying to cater to everyone's requirements was intensely challenging.

I wish I could say I got the balance right between time with the children being 'mum' and time with the children as 'teacher', but I was repeatedly discouraged by my own task-focused activity. It was a battle to put the academic pressures aside and simply concentrate on play, particularly with my youngest. When I did, the reward was great: Joel's spectacular smile eclipsed even the brightness of South Sudan's sunshine.

Homeschool was an ongoing learning experience: for me, for Esther, for Ben and for Joel. We fumbled along, learning day by day to work together, to play together. I was constantly adjusting our system to make it work better. I wondered what I could do to help me act with more understanding as I fought against my own impatience, my task-orientated focus, my lack of grace.

'I'm going to imagine there's a CCTV camera in the corner of the classroom where everyone can see our lessons,' I told the children one morning, pointing to a spot on the ceiling by the air-conditioning unit. I reasoned that if our supporters and friends could theoretically watch our homeschool, perhaps it would remind me to speak and act more like a professional teacher, rather than an irritated parent?

We gradually discovered that learning together can be lots of fun; that the satisfaction of finished work was a happiness shared. We got to know each other, with all our best traits and our warts, in a way that can never be recaptured. Because of the R and R (Rest and Relaxation) cycle, I was determined to use our time in Juba for school. We could then completely relax on our weeks away in Kenya and leave schoolwork firmly behind. This meant we only had a few days off school during each of our twelve weeks in Juba. It was busy; it was intense – yet this period of concentrated time together created a unique and valuable bond.

There was one challenge, though, that brought an extra layer to homeschooling in Juba. It was a challenge that stretched me and taught me more than I expected – and ultimately illustrated that when I am unable and inadequate, God never is.

29

God's enabling

'I hate reading!' Ben's normally cheerful face was twisted into a scowl as he pushed the book away. I pushed it back. We needed to keep trying, even though reading was such an unpleasant chore for my middle child.

Ben is articulate, has a fantastic memory for facts and recalls stories and things I have said long after I have forgotten them. He is bright, funny, enthusiastic in scientific tasks and full of brilliant and practical ideas. Yet learning letter names, reading books and certain aspects of mathematical learning were more challenging for Ben than for his peers. Recalling my teaching days in London where some of my students faced similar challenges, I started to wonder whether dyslexia might be making particular learning areas more difficult for my clever boy.

One afternoon, a comment of Ben's served to confirm my suspicions. We sat together, the school reading book open on the table in front of us. Ben screwed up his eyes, rubbed them hard with the back of his hand, then squealed in frustration. 'The page is too bright, Mummy,' he complained, 'and the letters keep jumping.'

'What do you mean, Ben?' I asked.

'The letters keep changing places and the page is all shiny – I can't read it.' He pouted, looking up at me with frustrated eyes.

Ben had just given me insight into the challenge he faced every time he was asked to read. If ever there was an indication of dyslexia, this was it: letters moving about, or 'visual stress', and struggling with light reflections. However, at six years old, Ben was too young for a formal assessment. Most recommendations advise waiting until a child is eight, allowing the student time to make progress.

While we therefore waited, I taught. While I taught, I discovered how inadequate my skills were. I had the knowledge to identify dyslexia, but for all my years of teaching experience, my knowledge about how to teach in a way that was dyslexia-friendly was shockingly lacking. I realised that I lacked the right resources. I knew I needed more understanding to tailor Ben's lessons to teach him effectively and missed having colleagues who could share their expertise of this subject. I keenly felt the absence of an educational support network.

Ben's UK tutor tried her best to help but was doubtful of my fears for Ben. He was young, she reminded me. Give him time, she said – but she had never met or worked with Ben. I was frustrated that she doubted my feedback. I was doubly stressed because this was my son and I felt so much love and responsibility for him. As his mum *and* his teacher, I wanted to do my utmost best to educate him. Instead, I felt like I was failing him.

One thing I could do was pray. I cried out before God, telling Him how inadequate I felt and about my fears that I was ruining Ben's education. I also cried on Andrew's shoulder. Other mothers sympathised, but they could not relate, making it a lonely experience. However, over time, I saw how God heard our prayers, not through a quick-fix solution, but through step-by-step help. One step at a time, He was providing answers and help, working out details for both Ben's good and to teach me to trust Him.

Initially, God sent professional help across my path when Mum gave me the contact details for Christine, who had a wealth of experience in teaching dyslexic students. Christine lived in the far-off English town of Burscough, so we made a plan to meet during our family UK home assignment in 2015. Christine took time to listen and heard me in a way nobody else had. As I explained our challenges with reading, spelling and number patterns, Christine understood and opened my eyes to a wealth of helpful resources. She steered me through two excellent websites that provided appropriate resources and information: The British Dyslexia Association and the Dyslexia Action organisation.

In England, we took Ben for a comprehensive eye test to see if he needed glasses to help him read. He didn't.

However, the test results did suggest that we should try coloured overlays on any texts that Ben read. This might help to reduce visual stress, the optician told us. Having tried a whole range of colours, it transpired that green overlays calmed the letter movement, making it easier for Ben to focus on decoding the words on the page. I ordered a pack and was pleased to observe that they helped Ben to read with more fluency.

Another huge help was a teacher's course – Struggling Readers and Writers by Osiris Educational – which I undertook in London on that same UK visit. Thankful to be granted a place on it, I picked up greater understanding of the challenges Ben faced and strategies to counteract them. I now knew more about how Ben learnt. It was an effective way to equip me for returning to our Juba schoolroom. On our journey back there, my suitcase was laden with literacy and mathematical supplies suitable for teaching Ben in a more relevant way.

I had been thrown a lifeline. The choppy waters of doubt in my ability to teach, of professional isolation and of inappropriate resources were being calmed. My confidence was being restored, just as Ben's increased. We celebrated every step of progress. Ben's star chart on the schoolroom wall filled rapidly with colourful stickers as Ben was rewarded for each book he read, reflecting the brighter outlook in our schoolroom.

In June 2016, we finally took Ben for an official educational assessment in Nairobi. Two extensive days of tests confirmed dyslexia. There were lots of helpful recommendations and practical ideas. The official report also meant that any future schools had a record of how best to support Ben's learning.

Best of all, however, was the kindness of Ms Davey in her assessment. She spent time going over her detailed report with me and Andrew, then related how well Ben had done in his learning. An experienced professional, she leaned in towards me across her vast, wooden desk, sincere tears glimmering at the corner of her eyes, and spoke her encouragement loud and clear: 'Liz, I have to tell you, being homeschooled is honestly the best thing that could have happened to Ben. The progress he has made and the confidence he has in his skills could not have been gained without the intense attention that is possible in a homeschool environment.

I was stunned – and delighted. I glanced over at Andrew with a smile.

I was relieved to know that Ben was doing well and that the approach we had taken was working. Her words were like a healing balm from God's First Aid Kit, smoothing over those bumpy scratches where I had felt overwhelmed, ill-equipped and inadequate. It was as though He was applying an ointment of reassurance, letting me know that placing Ben in a homeschool environment and appointing me as Ben's teacher for these two years was no mistake. Hadn't He told me back in September 2013, on our first Juba visit, that He doesn't make mistakes (Deuteronomy 32:4)?

I was seeing again that, despite my doubts in me, God *was* working all things out well for Ben and our family.

He was trustworthy. I thought that I had been discovering more about teaching and about dyslexia over these past two years, but in actual fact I was discovering more about God's faithfulness.

30

Pilot Parker at work

The sun sat low, a red ball suspended in the blue-tinged eastern sky. The long grass behind me glowed golden with the first rays of the sun, still gentle in the early morning. I enjoyed these moments, knowing that this ball of fire would soon rise higher to become a blazing furnace, its heat permeating the land.

The natural beauty behind me was in stark contrast to the man-made world of machines facing me. I stood on the tarmac of Juba International Airport, watching the buzz of activity. A large UN cargo plane was being prepared. Clouds of red dust billowed as its engines sprang to life. With a huge roar, it began to lumber down the taxiway to line up for take-off, like a beast on a mission. An equally enormous helicopter, the letters IGAD (Intergovernmental Authority on Development) painted on its side, had rolled slowly past on the ground a few minutes earlier before taking off. It was already a speck in the sky, its powerful rotor blades spinning forcefully. Nearby, I could see bands of busy workers preparing MSF (Médecins Sans Frontières) and WFP (World Food Programme) planes. The international relief effort kept Juba airport busy.

However, I was most interested in the well-dressed pilot directly in front of me. This was my handsome husband, preflighting his Cessna Caravan 208 MAF plane. Today, I had the fantastic privilege of joining him. I watched as the fuel truck drove across the tarmac to fill the tanks of the plane and as the dispatch team loaded up cargo, including 18 kilograms of eggs and other generous supplies. Soon, Andrew invited the passengers aboard. I was excited to join Pilot Parker in the cockpit and dutifully put on my headset. Andrew lined the aeroplane up – we were ninth in the queue for take-off, positioned behind a massive, noisy helicopter. Eventually, Andrew pushed the throttle forward and our plane began to gather speed, zipping along the runway and finally rising into the blue skies of South Sudan, soaring over the River Nile and beginning our journey to rural Kuron.

South Sudan is beautiful. I loved every minute of the flight, feasting my eyes on the scenery and enjoying the sight of the plane's shadow sliding over the treetops beneath. The lush landscape of the Sudd gave way to a wide forest, spread out like a thick carpet in varying shades of green, until Andrew finally started to line up the aircraft for our descent. We came in to land on Kuron's airstrip, a neat band of dirt cut out among the grass.

Bishop Paride Taban was the most well-known passenger on that flight. A gracious and dignified gentleman, he had devoted his life to serving others. As the dark-skinned, white-haired bishop alighted, a group of excited villagers gathered with obvious delight to welcome him home to Holy Trinity Peace Village. One older lady greeted him with a joyful dance, festooned in a bright orange blanket, her green, blue and red necklaces bobbing as she leapt. On her upper arm, she wore white beaded bracelets, while a double headband of red and blue beads added to her striking appearance. More white beads fashioned into a large loop made up her lip ring. Diagonal scars etched across her cheeks showed the tribe to which she belonged.

Holy Trinity Peace Village is an inspiring practical centre of vocational training and education, focused on encouraging unity in the local communities. Bishop Taban founded the centre based on his dream 'of a community where people with different ethnicity and different religious backgrounds can live side by side with confidence in harmony and fellowship', as its website proudly announces. The main project is empowering the local community to work the land better, providing them with enough food. The second goal is to help make education 'accessible and acceptable' for both boys and girls.

I felt honoured when the bishop took a firm hold of my arm and invited me to stand hand in hand with him for a photograph. We lined up next to his smiling assistant in her long, patterned African dress and a

Norwegian visitor, an investor in the Peace Village. As the photographer snapped us next to the MAF plane, I felt both humbled and privileged to be here with MAF. I saw for myself how it played a part in helping visions become a reality, providing safe transport in and out of this place so hard to reach by road.

The children at the airstrip gathered around us inquisitively. Some were dressed in a simple cloth. Some wore nothing but a beaded necklace. I showed them pictures of my white-skinned children and they screamed in amusement. Meeting white adult foreigners was one thing, but the images of white children roughly their age elicited excited chatter, though I couldn't understand a word. They posed seriously for photographs – I could not get them to share their radiant smiles – and enjoyed seeing their own images on the screen of the digital camera. I now also had some photographs to show Esther, Ben and Joel of their peers, living in such a different context.

Heavy rains had rendered the dirt roads from the airstrip to the main building slippery and difficult to navigate. This meant that Andrew and I could not take up the kind invitation to join the group setting off in a jeep for lunch at the Peace Village. Although the actual village was not far from the airstrip, those who had come to collect the bishop from the plane told us that the journey each way on such a muddy surface would take at least forty-five minutes. The total time involved in sharing lunch with our new friends could therefore have caused a serious delay to the MAF flight back into Juba.

Reluctantly, I bade farewell to the children, the dancing lady, the bishop and his team. While Andrew began to prepare the plane for its return flight, I took a few extra minutes to enjoy the vast open space around us and breathe in the unpolluted air of rural South Sudan, before the loud rumble of the engine drowned out the peace and quiet. As Andrew began to bring the plane to life, I clambered up the metal steps and back into the cockpit to fasten my seatbelt. The sun beat through the glass of the windshield while Andrew, at the controls, spoke calmly into the radio and turned us back in the direction of Juba. This day had been fascinating and exciting for me – I wanted to savour the moments of experiencing the work of MAF first-hand – but for Andrew this was just another day's work.

Andrew's South Sudan flights were not always so peaceful, though. When a location suddenly became insecure, MAF were sometimes called upon to evacuate staff members of NGOs. Tension would start with the first phone call, when the pilot began to feel the responsibility involved and to weigh up the risk factor. This tangible stress impacted the family as we sensed his distraction.

Once the pilot had left and was in the air, I became the one who was distracted. The relief when I heard that Andrew had landed safely back in Juba was like the lifting of a heavy cloak from around my shoulders. Other times, Andrew would return home to relate tales of encounters with less than friendly military personnel at certain airstrips – and then I was happy that I was only hearing about this with Andrew sitting safely beside me in our house.

I smiled when Andrew told me, on another occasion, about a group of soldiers in their camouflage uniforms who gathered around the MAF plane when it landed at a remote airstrip. Andrew was surprised and delighted when they started to help him unload the heavy sacks of grain, their backs bent under the load. After a few minutes, they asked Andrew, 'How much will you pay us for carrying these?' Good humouredly, Andrew laughed and replied that he could not pay them. Instantly, they stopped helping. Andrew found himself unloading the rest of the heavy cargo by himself while the soldiers sat around nearby under the hot sun and watched him hard at work. The scene was captured in a poignant photograph. The soldiers were simply looking for an opportunity to earn cash – but this was something MAF was not there to do.

MAF could and did provide help in many other ways. I love looking through the photographs and video footage taken during Andrew's flights in South Sudan. There are images of the MAF plane loaded up with building materials for medical or church projects in difficult-to-access locations, or materials needed to establish much-needed water wells. On some flights, the aeroplane was jam-packed with boxes of Plumpy'nut, a food supplement destined for feeding centres where malnourished children were nursed back to health. On other flights, boxes of soap were headed to Motot for a Tearfund project to improve hygiene in remote villages, helping to prevent disease.

In one photograph, through the open door of the plane you see piles of bicycles. These were taken to a remote corner of South Sudan to allow health workers a faster means of transport than travelling by foot, enabling them to care for more patients on a daily basis. Sometimes, the MAF plane carried stacks of Bibles in local languages to bring an accessible gift of hope to isolated people. They received their Bibles with great celebrations and singing, elated to finally be able to read God's word in their own language. Some photographs are more sombre, illustrating the times when the MAF plane carried medical patients. During medical evacuation flights, sick passengers were strapped on to stretchers, secured to the floor of the plane, so as to get them to Juba for hospital treatment as quickly as possible.

Occasionally, it was a coffin that was being transported. Family members or friends soberly surrounded the wooden casket as it winged its way from Juba back to the person's home village for burial, honouring a widespread cultural tradition about where the final resting places should be. The photographs Andrew showed me were humbling, with mourners gathered round the plane on the dusty airstrip, taking consolation from the fact that they could now grieve together as a community and find closure as they prepared for the funeral.

One day, I pushed open the small door into the refreshingly cool, air-conditioned operations office on our Juba compound. I blinked as my eyes adjusted from the bright sunshine outside to the array of screens and technical equipment which tracked the aeroplanes and connected MAF pilots to a central hub of information.

In contrast to the high-tech equipment, there was an old-fashioned cork board mounted on a nearby wall on which cards were pinned up. Intrigued, I stepped closer to read thank-you notes that had been sent to MAF South Sudan. Some were from individuals, some from groups, and others came from NGOs and organisations. They all shouted out the same message – that MAF had made a positive impact, bringing practical help and encouragement at a time of need.

I smiled. It was good to be reminded that God was using MAF to bring hope, help and His love right here in South Sudan.

31

The stark reality of poverty

'Khawaja! Khwaja!' The little girl was screaming and pointing at me and Ben as we made our way into the small corner shop, looking for milk powder to buy. Abruptly, she burst into tears and ran to hide behind a tall, dark lady in a long, blue dress. The lady laughed and picked up the child, then launched into a string of words in Juba-Arabic that I could not understand. I knew what *'Khawaja'* meant, though. It was a word used to refer to foreigners with white skins. She placed the child on the shop counter and laughed louder when the child tried to hide again. Ben grinned at me, aware of the drama we were creating in this shop.

Some people in Juba were not used to seeing white faces. This tiny girl, no more than three years old, was terrified by our appearance. Feeling embarrassed, I hurriedly bought a tin of milk powder and returned home.

Being different often attracted attention. If I walked with my children in the street, other children approached, their hands outstretched as they asked for money and help. We made it a priority to carry food with us so that we had something to give, rather than offering money which may be used to fuel unhelpful habits. Sometimes they wanted to touch my children's blond hair or light skin because it was different from theirs.

Once, I encountered a boy with oozing sores on his leg, so I tried to find out how to get him some first aid. When I mentioned this to another MAF lady, she said they had tried to help him, several times, but he always pulled any dressings off and used a sharp stone to reopen the wound.

'Why does he do that?' I asked, shocked.

'It's more profitable to beg if you have an open wound,' she replied.

It was horrible to know that so many kids in Juba were living in intense poverty, as in any city in the developing world. It was an age-old dilemma, not knowing how to alleviate the overwhelming poverty we saw in the African cities where we lived. One organisation we had links with in Juba was Confident Children Out of Conflict (often referred to as CCC; www.confidentchildren.org). They offered shelter, education, rehabilitation and, most importantly, love to the children of Juba – children who had to cope not just with poverty, but with war crimes, loss of their families and sometimes abuse of the worst kinds. The work of CCC was impressive.

We met many individuals in Juba who inspired us with their commitment to care for and love others in the name of Jesus. One Dutch couple at MAF organised local distribution of food parcels at Christmas. This was an annual gift to the poorest of the poor, many of whom lived in makeshift shacks created out of iron sheets, tarpaulins, cardboard or random pieces of wood and hastily erected in the grounds of Juba cemetery. It was a desolate place – filthy, overcrowded, with no running water, no electricity, no security – and desperately sad to see.

A few days before Christmas, the children and I joined many members of the MAF team, along with staff and some of the children from CCC, to prepare these food parcels. We sat outdoors measuring cups of dried beans, sugar, tea leaves and salt, making sure each one was exactly the same. The South Sudanese children raised their energetic voices and burst into spontaneous song as they worked, establishing a joyful rhythm for us all. It was such a huge undertaking that it took two days to get everything organised. Before the distribution, a team of people were sent into the community to give a card to each household in need. People were reminded to bring this with them on distribution day and exchange it for a bag filled with the staple foods and necessities like milk powder, charcoal, oil and laundry soap. The card exchange was an ingenious system to avoid missing anyone out or creating conflict by accidentally giving some families more than others.

It was Christmas Eve when the volunteers set off to actually hand out of the parcels. Andrew and I decided to take Esther, Ben and Joel with us. We knew we would be working in teams, spilt up to cover different areas. Joel stuck close to his dad and the older two stayed with a team visiting the outskirts of the cemetery. My group was sent to the main part of the cemetery. We drove up the dusty track next to the cemetery, parked our vehicles and climbed through a gap in a smashed brick wall. We then took up our places on the gritty, sandy ground in the midst of this informal, disorganised settlement. The unpleasant odour of rotting rubbish alerted my senses even more keenly to the poverty within these tumbledown walls.

A truck, loaded with piles of food parcels, had accompanied us and was positioned just outside the broken wall. We stood ready to act as a human conveyor belt, with volunteers passing the parcels from the truck to the front of the line as masses of people arrived to collect their Christmas gift. The line of recipients stretched back further than I could see, a long column of adults, but I was impressed at the orderly queue as people shuffled forward. One by one, they were pleased to reach the front and exchange their card for a yellow plastic bag filled with essential goods.

Children with distended bellies, many of them barely clothed, hopped and ran around the outskirts of the line, their eyes wide with curiosity at this unusual event. I noticed a couple of ladies staggering under the influence of alcohol, their eyes unfocused. One of them lurched forward, tried to grab my arm and leaned in to speak to me, her breath smelling of beer and her words incomprehensible. Alarmed, I took a step back, then directed her to a place in the queue. My heart went out to the children for whom this was just their ordinary life, but I felt for the mothers too. *It must be so tough to be a mother in this environment,* I thought, as I handed a plastic bag of goods to another mum with a baby strapped on her back.

On the one hand, the need was overwhelming. On the other hand, the generosity of the organisation behind this initiative was inspiring. While intricate, patterned scars cut into people's foreheads indicated their different tribal groups, today those distinctions didn't matter. They all had a common purpose as they waited for their little package, given from a big heart of compassion.

Sometimes, we met world changers who visited South Sudan from overseas, influencing us for the better with their tireless work to alleviate suffering. Occasionally, these people were well-known names in the political arena – one of whom I was delighted to meet unexpectedly on the streets of Juba. On a routine Monday afternoon, the children and I were walking home from our weekly swim at Landmark Hotel. Refreshed by the cool waters of the swimming pool, we walked uncharacteristically quickly in the afternoon heat. I found myself catching up with two foreign ladies who were strolling down the street ahead of us. As I got closer, I heard two distinctly

British accents. Intrigued to meet fellow Brits in our neighbourhood, I increased my pace to draw alongside and introduce myself.

The lady on the right, with short, dark hair cut just above her shoulders, looked familiar and just as I was about to speak, I recognised her face: she was Baroness Cox. I was amazed to see this well-known politician, a member of the British House of Lords, and someone I respect for her charity work. An influential lady, she uses her position to fight for the rights of oppressed people across the globe. A few months earlier, in January 2015, Andrew had carried her as one of his passengers when she visited a remote area of South Sudan in conjunction with her charity work. We have a photo of Andrew and Baroness Cox standing in front of the MAF plane. I asked Andrew to tell her how much I appreciate her incredible work, but today she was walking right next to me. I could tell her myself.

I smiled and took a breath, but before I could speak, Baroness Cox looked over and smiled back. Encouraged, I burst out excitedly, 'Baroness Cox, it's lovely to meet you! I know you don't know me, but you flew in a MAF plane recently and my husband was your pilot.' I told her how much I admired her work in South Sudan and worldwide, and for being a voice for the voiceless through her charity HART (The Humanitarian Aid Relief Trust). This works relentlessly to provide aid and advocacy for victims of oppression and persecution. She was gracious, down to earth and approachable, and we talked for a few more minutes. Then the children and I turned down our side street to head back home.

I was still excited when I burst through our front door and called for Andrew. 'Guess who I just met?' I shouted.

The Baroness Cox was one of many charitable workers who passed through Juba. Save the Children, Samaritan's Purse, the Red Cross, Tearfund, Oxfam and WaterAid were just a few of the numerous charities that had a visible presence in Juba, some of whom flew regularly with MAF. Despite the sad effects of decades of war and the ensuing poverty, it was humbling to witness the efforts of so many to bring relief and healing.

For Esther, Ben and Joel, the reality of poverty is a fact they have grown up with – an awareness that I hope will inspire acts of compassion and justice. This understanding has developed through incidents like the following. One Saturday morning, Andrew and I felt like a change of scenery away from our compound, so we borrowed one of the MAF cars and drove to Afex River Camp on the banks of the Nile (a hotel complex of large tents and prefabricated buildings). Once we arrived, Esther, Ben and Joel played near the bushes on the riverside and admired the half-sunken boat that was sticking up out of the water at a strange angle. Suddenly, the children spotted a group of naked children and a group of naked men washing themselves in the river, while their clothes dried on bushes nearby. At first, Esther was appalled.

'Esther,' I asked her gently, 'where would you wash if you didn't have a bathroom? And what would you wear when you washed your clothes, if you only have one outfit?'

She stared at me as if a lightbulb had been turned on in her head. Then she turned back to her game and never batted an eyelid at such scenes again.

32

The chained patient

On the dirty floor, the man, just skin and bones, writhed in agonising pain and pulled once again at the metal cuffs binding his ankles to the legs of the metal hospital bed. His strength was low and his eyes, sunken in what was left of his face, emanated a hopelessness that shocked me. This was almost as disturbing as the mess of bloody skin and tissue which hung limply where his jaw had once been and the open sores oozing puss at his throat.

Suddenly, a tall, dark lady in a long, blue dress strode boldly up the ward towards where his bed was. She stopped in front of the patient on the floor and stared openly, curious but strangely unfeeling. The man tried in vain to hide his shame, pulling a worn piece of *kanga* from under his scant frame and draping it over his head. The gaudy rainbow colours of the cloth did little to conceal him from the inquisitive gaze.

I was appalled. I had never witnessed a patient in such squalor, I had never seen such open and oozing wounds, and I had never seen a patient cuffed by his ankles to a hospital bed.

Ward five of Juba Teaching Hospital was one of the most uncomfortable places I have visited. It was an emergency ward, but lack of hygiene and care made it clear that the ward itself needed an emergency injection of cash. The fetid smell hit me before the sight of abandoned, bloodied cotton wool swabs littering the dirt-streaked floor. Frenzied flies buzzed over the open wounds of patients sitting or lying on sagging mattresses, some of which did not even have sheets.

On our way in, I had stepped around an old man lying listlessly on the floor on soiled bedding, curled up in a foetal position, his empty eyes staring at the dirty concrete wall. At the nurse's station just along the corridor, two nurses bursting out of tight, white uniforms sat in front of a desk where a black-and-white TV crackled. Colourful plastic cups half filled with water or black tea rested on unsteady nightstands between beds.

That Friday morning we were supposed to be visiting Susan, one of the beautiful South Sudanese ladies who gently cared for two of the MAF families on our compound. She had been shot on Wednesday night when armed thieves broke into her home. In their unfortunately successful attempt to steal her brother's motorbike, they had resorted to using guns. Now Susan was lying helplessly on a rickety bed in the Juba Teaching Hospital.

Blood oozed through the bandages wrapped around the wound where a bullet had torn into the top of her left leg. Thankfully her prognosis was good – the bullet had not damaged any essential organs – but it would be a while before she could walk freely again.

Just a few days earlier, Susan had played the part of Mary in our MAF staff Christmas play. Andrew and another pilot had made incongruous but surprisingly effective angels, dressed in fetching white sheets and tinsel halos. It had been a festive and happy celebration. Yet there was nothing jolly about this unexpected hospital visit just four days later.

Three of us MAF ladies – Dagmar, Karyn and I – joined Susan's friends and relatives gathered around her bed. She was attached to a drip administering much-needed pain relief. Yet even under pressure, Susan amazed me with her smile, and humbled us with her acceptance of what had been a terrifying ordeal and with her will to recover. Susan was one of the luckier patients, with people to care for her, to provide bedding for the stained, plastic-covered mattress, and to bring her food. Given how gifted she was at caring for others, it was good to see that others were now caring for her.

The tortured patient situated across the ward from Susan's bed had no such luck. Nobody was looking after his needs. Despite being appalled by his condition, I couldn't help my attention being drawn again and again to his desperate plight. I wondered why he was chained up with handcuffs around his ankles. My friend Dagmar was bolder than I, though. She determinedly crossed the ward to speak to him after our conversation with Susan.

'Good morning. How are you?' she began.

I hated to admit it, but I was fearful of approaching him. I had been torn between wanting to speak with him and recoiling with fear at his condition. However, seeing Dagmar's initiative inspired me. Dagmar crouched down at his eye level and attempted conversation. At first, his eyes registered suspicion, but this was replaced by co-operation as Dagmar's kindness shone through. This was maybe the first dignified opportunity he had been offered in a while.

A hospital worker was called over to help translate what was a difficult conversation. The English language wasn't the only barrier. Speech was also impeded by the fact that his jaw was shot to pieces and that red-raw, festering flaps of skin hung limply where half of his mouth should be.

Haltingly, the hospital worker helped to piece together the jigsaw of his ugly story. I understood a tale of HIV infection, of drunkenness, of murder and ultimately of attempted suicide once he realised he could not undo the shooting of his child. He had aimed the gun at his head, attempting to kill himself. A conscious-stricken friend tried to stop him, forcefully smacking the gun out of the way as it exploded. The result was not only a face blown to pieces, a jaw that was blown to smithereens and a throat that hung open, but a heart that was broken and a painful conscience that could not be relieved. Now he was chained like a fugitive though too weak to escape, waiting for treatment until he was fit enough to be transferred to prison.

Splashed on the squalid tiles around his bed were puddles of water. Each time he attempted to drink, the liquid poured out of that hole in his throat and dribbled, unchecked, down his thin chest and on to the floor. It was exhausting, disheartening and tragic.

As we prepared to leave ward five, Dagmar spoke gently to the tormented young man and told him clearly that *nothing* stops God's forgiveness and love. She made sure the message was translated.

When we left, I think I saw a glimmer of hope in his eyes – those pools of torment. I was impressed by Dagmar's courage and thankful that she had been able to give a simple but profound message to somebody in intense suffering.

33
Hope instead of horror

One week later, Dagmar, Karyn and I ventured back to ward five to visit Susan. It was a stifling, humid Christmas Eve and sweat clung to me as we walked across the hospital compound. Ward five was still hectic, with clusters of relatives gathered around the beds of the many patients, but we were taken aback to find Susan's bed occupied by a different patient. Opposite, the man with the tragic tale was still cuffed to his bed, but had now covered himself with his cloth and was simply a hulking form on the filthy tiles.

There were no staff members around to ask where Susan was, so we decided to head outside and call her on her mobile phone. As we exited the ward, two young men with bleeding head wounds and limp bodies were hastily carried past us, apparently by their friends who had unloaded them off a trailer attached to a motorbike. The injured men were laid on mattresses on the floor. I tried not to look, but found that my legs were shaking as I passed first them and then the overflowing, lidless bin, stuffed with discarded medical gloves, used needles and stained cotton wool. Ward five continued to feel oppressive with overwhelming needs – and I hated the way I couldn't make it better. After the smell of sickness clung to me inside the building, I was thankful to be out in the open air again, even in the humidity.

When we called Susan's phone, though, there was good news. We discovered that friends had helped her walk up to ward three – a recovery ward a few minutes away. Her recovery was going well!

Crossing the open space between the single-storey wards, we encountered several groups of relatives who had set up rough camping areas on the sparse grass of the hospital grounds to cook meals for the patients they knew. Without the care of friends and relatives, hospital recovery would be either a hungry or an expensive experience. Only wealthy patients could afford to buy food from the hospital café.

Ward three was a welcome contrast to ward five – it had high ceilings, mosquito netting covering the open windows and large ceiling fans helping to circulate air. It was a peaceful and healthier place to recuperate. Susan smiled a welcome. She was lying down and in pain, but making a steady recovery, and with friends or relatives in constant attendance. We left reassured, seeing that she was in a better ward and in kind hands.

However, I continued to think of the prisoner-patient in ward five and felt bad for him as we returned to our homes later that afternoon. His dreadful condition disturbed my spirit. In the blackness of the Juba night, I lay still, staring up into the darkness, asking what we could do to help and praying for God's help and mercy over him.

Two weeks later, my friend Carolyn, one of Joel's teachers, returned with me to the hospital. We went to see Susan first and were delighted to find her now standing up and starting to walk independently. Her recovery was a positive testimony to the dedication of the medical staff at Juba Teaching Hospital and to Susan's caring friends. She beamed at us and we were delighted to see her almost ready to be discharged.

Buoyed up by this good news, we set off down the concrete path to visit the man in dire straits on ward five. This time, the ward was quieter. After making our way down the ward, we discovered that somebody had placed the man's mattress on the floor underneath him, so that he was no longer scooting about the floor in distress. He had a drip being fed into his arm and the skin flaps under his face had been stitched back into place, restoring the shape of his jaw. Since his mouth and throat still had large gaps, communication wasn't straightforward, but he seemed pleased to have visitors. When we asked if we could pray with him, he made the sign of the cross and nodded. We squatted next to him and prayed. Next, Carolyn helped to tip some water into his open mouth as he lay back on his mattress – this helped to make more liquid go down. He then pointed to his stomach, signalling hunger.

I looked at Carolyn. How were we going to feed him if he had such difficulty swallowing? Anyway, we had no food.

Carolyn had a great idea. 'Let's walk over to that café by the entrance and see what's on offer,' she suggested.

We found this at the edge of the hospital compound. Spotting bowls of stew which looked like a kind of soup, we purchased some and then deliberately forced it into a plastic bottle, before returning with this to the hungry patient.

This started a trend. For the next month, Carolyn and another MAF colleague, Rob, faithfully visited the man, who told us his name was Wieu-Wieu. Three times a week, they took him a plastic bottle filled with soup, which we took turns to make and liquidise. They also brought water, clothes, soap and a Bible in Arabic, and spent time sitting by him, talking and simply being his friend. I only visited once more with Carolyn, not bold enough to visit more often. However, I had written about his story on my blog, which had prompted some of our supporters to join us in praying for him. Therefore, on the last visit, we once again prayed with him and were able to tell him that people as far off as England were praying for him too.

Wieu-Wieu wrote us a note in broken English that read, 'God is with you. God loves you. I love you friend.' He began to read his Bible and a new peace settled over him, even in his physical suffering. The torment I had seen in his eyes was replaced by something lighter – something that shone. Its name was hope.

In February, the time came for Wieu-Wieu to be transferred to a military hospital. We suspected he would ultimately be taken to prison. I wish I could tell you what happened after hospital, but I have no further news of him. His body was weakened by HIV, so the physical outlook was grim. However, we prayed that he would find a new purpose and ultimately make his peace with Jesus, the one who loved him enough to give up His life for him. Carolyn was filled with excitement. 'I'm so pleased that I'll get to see Wieu-Wieu in heaven!' she told me, full of faith that God would answer our prayers.

I had been deeply disturbed by my encounter with Wieu-Wieu. I had never seen such anguish in someone's eyes and it shook me to my core. However, through him I witnessed the chain reaction that can happen when God's people start with a simple act of kindness. Dagmar's initial act of speaking to a man in difficulty started a domino effect, bringing hope to one of God's troubled, but unforgotten, children. I saw the amazing and uplifting effect that can happen when loving Jesus is an action, not just a statement of faith.

34

A miracle in Juba

I don't believe in coincidence, and the events that were about to unfold confirmed my belief.

Joel rubbed his eyes for the umpteenth time that morning.

'Darling, don't rub so hard,' I chided him. His eyes were looking red and the area around his right eye was becoming swollen, making him squint.

'Is it itchy?' I asked again.

Four-year-old Joel shook his head.

Joel and Esther had both had nasty bouts of conjunctivitis when we lived in Dodoma, their eyes crusty, red and swollen, aggravated by the small particles of brown dust that floated constantly in the air. But Joel's problem was different – and a mystery. I had never seen a swelling like this and the redness was forming a ring around his eye socket, while there was no crusty mess around his eye.

Sue, a British nurse who was staying a few months on the MAF compound, had a look at Joel's eyes and wasn't sure what the infection was either. When Andrew came back from his flight late that Tuesday afternoon, he took Joel in a MAF vehicle to a local clinic around the corner.

The small, dark clinic was oppressively warm but thankfully not too busy when they arrived. After a short wait, they were ushered into the room where the tall South Sudanese doctor did a brief examination of Joel's eyes.

'Hmm, I think you just need to wash them with clean, warm water,' was his diagnosis.

Andrew bundled Joel into the MAF pick-up – which was now baking having been parked in the hot sun of the stony car park – and drove the short distance back to our Hai Cinema compound.

'I don't think washing his eyes is going to help,' I commented to Andrew when he told me the doctor's advice. 'It might even make them worse – we've already tried washing them and his eyes are getting redder every day!' My voice began to rise as I felt the stress of not knowing how to help my son.

That evening, I felt so concerned by the continued problem that I decided to email a doctor at London's Interhealth Clinic. I had already taken some photos of the increasing redness and swelling around Joel's eye, as he stood squinting at the camera in the Juba sunshine. I duly attached them to the email with my questions. The doctor surprised me by getting back to me unusually quickly. Their website explains that replies can take up to twenty-four hours, but I barely had to wait for a response. He seemed concerned by the photographs and suggested that perhaps the problem was blepharitis, an inflammation of the eyelid. He recommended a certain antibiotic eye cream. The challenge would be trying to find that specific cream in a nearby pharmacy – but at least we could try.

I sensed an urgency in dealing with the situation. Joel was miserable and, although there was no fever or itching, the area around his eye was increasingly sensitive. The problem was making him tired and subdued. While it was too late to get the antibiotic medicine today, I planned a pharmacy trip in the morning. Thankfully, friends were willing to supervise the children on the compound and Sue was willing to come and search the pharmacies of Juba with me. Andrew had a hectic flight schedule that day, so it was good to have neighbours to call on while he was busy.

Sue and I set off into the warmth of Wednesday morning, striding the streets as we sought out the eye cream. I was so grateful for Sue's calm, reassuring friendship and presence. It was an advantage to be with an experienced nurse who could reliably check the ingredients of the cream. It felt like we walked for miles across the developed area of the city. Several of the chemists were tiny, with cramped, wooden shelves and limited supplies. Their tired-looking staff barely raised their heads from their phone screens when we pushed open the doors to come in, and they spoke little English. Other pharmacies were air-conditioned and better stocked, with clean tiles and glass counters displaying a multitude of medical goods. All of them had one thing in common: they did not stock the cream we were looking for.

Disappointed, hot and sweating, we returned home, wondering what to do next. I planned to email the London doctor to explain that I could not find the cream for blepharitis and ask for advice. However, a surprise was in store as I opened my computer screen. A new email was flashing at me from Dr Helen, a British doctor. She had supervised our family's medical on our last UK visit, at the same London Interhealth Clinic. Her colleague, whom I had emailed yesterday evening, had explained our situation to her. It just so happened that Dr Helen was in Juba this very Wednesday, leading a medical training event for an NGO – and she was willing to examine Joel's eyes at lunchtime.

I pushed back my office chair in haste and rushed across to the MAF offices to see if anyone was available to drive me and Joel to where Dr Helen was leading her training event – at the Afex River Camp compound across town. Colleague Rob was able to help out, so we made arrangements to set off as close to our lunch break as possible.

Once again, the MAF community rallied round, with friends taking Esther and Ben for lunch while Joel and I clambered into a MAF car with Rob as our chauffeur. Arriving in the burning heat of midday, the blissful air-conditioned reception area gave instant respite as we entered the slick interior of the first large tent. A smart, young receptionist was surprised to see us arrive with a small child, but was helpful. I hastily explained that Dr Helen was expecting us.

'She's busy leading the training right now,' the receptionist answered, 'but I will let her know you are here.'

We only had to wait a few minutes. Relief flooded over me as Dr Helen appeared through a small door. Here was a doctor I trusted. When caring for small children in a far-off land, that sense of relief cannot be underestimated. Helen smiled, then turned to Joel and looked at his eye closely, asking a few questions. She then asked me if I would step outside for a moment and please leave Joel indoors. Oh! This made me nervous. What did she need to say that Joel should not hear?

'Liz,' she began, 'I don't want to frighten you, but this is actually quite serious.'

Those words had a strange effect on me: I wanted to cry. No mother wants to hear that their child is dealing with a serious medical issue. However, I fought down that urge, made a big effort to concentrate and listened carefully. This was not a moment to crumble – it was a moment to take note of details.

Dr Helen went on to tell me that Joel had cellulitis around his eye. The official condition, she explained, was periorbital cellulitis. This is a bacterial infection around the eye which can lead to serious complications if not treated quickly with antibiotics. Helen continued to say that if Joel had been in England with these symptoms, he would have been in hospital on an IV drip to ensure he was getting the correct antibiotics. She explained that it was too late to try and get Joel to Nairobi for more advanced medical help, but two types of strong antibiotics, three times per day, would be a good treatment.

As we went back inside, I found that my legs were a little less steady than before, yet I was grateful for the clear medical advice. I crossed the reception area to sit with Joel, who was waiting on a chair, his small legs swinging a distance above the ground. My little boy, with his red and swollen face, looked so vulnerable. Helen took a piece of paper and started writing down several combinations of antibiotics and their correct dosage for a four-year-old child.

'If you can't get these, try the next ones on the list. Keep moving down the list depending on availability,' she told me. It was a comprehensive list that allowed for local medicine shortages. I was so thankful for the way Helen understood the environment we lived in and did not just assume that the first combination of antibiotics would automatically be in stock in Juba.

I thanked Helen profusely, but was keen to get to a pharmacy and start Joel's treatment. The sooner the better. I gathered Joel up and we followed Rob, who had kindly offered to drive us to the pharmacy as well, to the car park. Holding tightly to the list of antibiotics, I went inside the first chemist's but found that they did not have what was required. We parked outside a second pharmacy. They did not stock these antibiotics either.

By now, I was praying hard as we drove to the pharmacy across the road from Juba Teaching Hospital. Joel stayed safely in the air-conditioned car with Rob while I stepped into the hot city street and made my way to this third chemist's. Inside, I discovered a heaving mass of humanity. The pharmacy was about to close for lunch and patients, or relatives of patients, from the hospital were clamouring to get the appropriate medicines. Queues are not a normal procedure in South Sudan, so people were shouting across one another and waving prescriptions at the pharmacists behind the wooden counter. I suddenly felt very short among the taller South Sudanese crowd – and very desperate. Deciding I needed to be assertive to be seen, I brusquely pushed my way to the front and waved my paper as high as I could. I was thankful when a pharmacist took pity on me, grabbed the paper and pointed at the first two antibiotics on the list.

'We have these,' she said. 'Is this what you want?'

'Yes!' I was shouting in my enthusiasm and in my determination to be heard over the din of voices.

Within a few minutes, I emerged triumphantly from the pharmacy, clutching a paper bag containing the first two medicines that Dr Helen had listed. I breathed a prayer of gratitude as I belted myself back into the car. We drove the few minutes back to the compound and, after thanking Rob, I quickly took Joel indoors to feed him and get started on his treatment. I have never been so impatient to begin a course of medicine. I rushed to mix the antibiotic powder with clean water from our water filter and commenced

Joel's rigorous course of antibiotics. On a piece of paper I drew a timetable, then attached it to the wall, so that we would not forget a single dose.

I could barely wait for Andrew to come home so that I could tell him the whole story. I marvelled at how the timing lined up. Finding that cream for blepharitis would have been a hindrance rather than a help. It was amazing that Helen was there when we needed her medical expertise. It was brilliant that the best choice of antibiotics was available and that the pharmacy was still open when we got there. It was not simply coincidental that all those things lined up! God was looking after Joel.

Just a couple of days later, Joel's redness and swelling were visibly reduced. Joining friends for a meal at a restaurant, we were delighted to find Helen seated at a nearby table with colleagues, before her flight out of South Sudan. She checked Joel's progress in this unlikely environment and was pleased with how well he was responding to his antibiotics. What a bonus to have an unofficial check-up.

Many months later, I was on home assignment in England and visiting St Michael's Church in London's Belgravia. I was speaking at a meeting about God's grace to us during our time in Juba. I nodded to Sylvia, my friend who was manning the PowerPoint presentation for me, and she brought up the next image on the large white screen. It was a photo of an unhappy four-year-old boy with a swollen, red ring around his eye: Joel. I began to relate the story of God's faithfulness and His perfect timing.

After the talk, a lovely lady approached me. Although well-spoken, her voice could barely conceal her emotion as she spoke with me. 'Liz, when you say you saw a miracle in Joel's healing from periorbital cellulitis, I am not sure if you realise what a great miracle this actually was. My granddaughter had this same infection, here in London.'

The lady explained how the little girl was on a drip, unwell for months and moved from one hospital to another one as they battled the infection. It had been a long and difficult journey for the family, though happily her granddaughter was now fully recovered. 'We have the best hospitals here and great medical advice,' she continued, 'but you were in Juba, with two bottles of antibiotics and within days Joel was better. Truly, you saw a miracle. This is an amazing story of God's healing.'

We were both emotional now. How kind God had been to us – but it took me a trip across the world, to an encounter in London, to fully grasp how incredible His miracle really was.

35

The Promise-Keeper

I took a leap and plunged into the sparkling waters of the Landmark Hotel swimming pool. Bliss! That initial burst of cool water on my sun-roasted skin was so refreshing. Esther shrieked with delight, grabbed her friend's hand and splashed in next to me.

'Mummy, Mummy!' called Joel, eager to join in with the action, his arms outstretched as he reached for me to catch him. He, too, wanted to plunge into the inviting blue waters. Ben, meanwhile, was already exercising a feat of diving in the deep end of the pool, alongside his friend, Ethan.

Every Monday afternoon, we walked the ten-minute distance from our compound to swim at this large pool. The hot walk along baking pavements made the water even more appealing. However, the best part was meeting up with our friends. We had made these Monday afternoons a weekly fixture with another homeschooling family: French Nathalie, her South Sudanese husband and their three children. They had become good friends since their arrival in Juba to work for the organisation YWAM (Youth with a Mission).

Nathalie and I shared parenting and homeschooling ideas. Since Nathalie and I always conversed in French, I was able to improve the language I'd studied at university, but which had lain dormant too long. Her friendship proved to be a special gift. I always looked forward to time with faith-filled, wise Nathalie, with her sense of adventure, her sense of humour and her depth of care for other people.

We also met up every Friday afternoon, when Nathalie and her children jumped into a handy *tuk-tuk* (motorised rickshaw) outside their home across town to get a lift to our compound. She and I joined Canadian Kristen for a time of lively French conversation, then the three of us shared a time of prayer. Kristen and her family were preparing to move to French-speaking Madagascar, where her husband would continue to fly for MAF, so an afternoon of French conversation was great practice for her before their transition.

Our children rushed outside to play with other compound children in the safety of the playground, with its closed gates and secure boundaries. The gang of children in Juba was growing and my heart was thankful to see how God had kept His promise to do 'all things'. I was especially thankful that He had even provided a

French girl the same age as Esther to help her reconnect to her own age group. I had been aware that Esther spent most of her time playing with children much younger than herself. While I saw this growing a compassionate heart in my daughter, I had sometimes been concerned that Esther may forget how to relate to her peers.

I was equally thankful for the ladies on our MAF compound and the inspiring team and leaders surrounding us. It was hard to say goodbye when Kristen's family left for Madagascar and Dagmar's family returned to their native Holland. The children and I cried sorry tears as friends disappeared – again. This has always been part of our life with MAF. However, new people kept arriving. When Israeli-born Nadia and her family came to Juba one year after us, I quickly realised that God had sent me another treasure. Nadia and I became firm friends, helped by the fact that she had lived in Tanzania before South Sudan and therefore understood a little of our background with MAF.

Nadia and I spent many energising hours sharing our stories over cups of tea, or family meals. Both she and I are talkative, so it was a wonder either of us could get a word in sideways; there always seemed to be so much to say. Somehow, we both chatted and we both listened. Ever observant, Nadia saw the pressure I put myself under to prepare lessons in advance of each new school week. Excelling at hospitality, she offered to feed my children on Friday lunchtimes and give them an art lesson so that I could use that time for lesson planning.

What a massive help this was to me, carving out over two hours of time when I could hide in the schoolroom and make headway before I took time off to join Nathalie and Kristen for our Friday afternoon get-togethers. When I had a funny story, or when I needed a shoulder to cry on, Nadia's door was always open.

I had been given a true friend. Again, I saw that my fears of lack were unfounded. God, the Promise-Keeper, was doing what He always did – being true to His word.

The One who can do 'all things' sent numerous other blessings our way. Esther, Ben and Joel made special memories as they ran wild and free – and often muddy – across the playground. It was a joy to see them splashing in the small, round pool in the centre of the compound with a carefree bunch of kids or bouncing up and down on the trampoline. I was thankful that we had other children with whom we could celebrate birthdays. Esther's tenth birthday was a fun occasion – we decorated the house with home-made paper fish and seaweed for an 'under the sea' birthday party, played fish-themed games and ate fish-shaped cake before she and her guests went for a rather crowded swim in the overground pool.

Birthdays in Juba always left us with happy memories. Joel's fourth birthday party was centred around a dinosaur theme, although one of the tiny guests was terrified when Andrew appeared in a green dinosaur mask. Screeching in fear, the small child scuttled behind me, while the other little guests energetically pelted the 'monster' with water balloons. Joel's fifth birthday was a little harder to prepare for, as he insisted that he wanted a 'bumblebee' party. I wasn't quite sure what that might entail? With imagination, Nadia helped me create a bee-shaped cake, we made up some bee-themed games and Joel's young guests looked cute in yellow and black outfits.

Ben's eighth birthday was a more raucous affair, as we tailored it around his chosen 'pirates' theme. We handed out bottles of orange juice 'grog' to his guests, who then walked the plank over the paddling pool, fished for marshmallows on strings and ate bowls of jelly. I hid a selection of revolting plastic insects in the jelly, so the children screamed with disgust as they extracted them. Unfortunately for the air-conditioning repair man, he arrived just as Ben's party was getting underway. The unsuspecting worker recoiled in shock when I threw open the front door, resplendent in my pirate outfit: a bright-red bandana around my head, enormous, hooped earrings twinkling at my ears and my front teeth blacked out with eyeliner. It was only when he nervously stepped back that I realised how absurd I must have looked to a man accustomed to a sensible office environment. He did not know what to make of this crazy MAF lady!

At Christmas, there were fun gatherings – both larger events with the entire team of national and international staff, and smaller festivities on the compound as we approached Christmas Day. Just like the community in Dodoma, friends in Juba became like extended family. We relied on sharing significant occasions with one another.

'Carols by the Nile' was one of my favourite festive events. I found it moving to stand on the grassy banks of that mighty, ancient river, singing about the Christmas story whose origins were older than the River Nile itself. Crickets and frogs competed for attention over the sound of human voices, but they were drowned out by the enthusiastic singing. The adults smiled indulgently as the young children from Joel's preschool sang a rendition of 'Away in a Manger'. The sun set rapidly, as it always does in Africa, allowing pretty coloured fairy lights to twinkle in the darkness of the humid evening.

The melodious singing of the MAF national staff at their morning devotions was another aspect I loved about our Juba life. Rich, energetic African voices rang out in song just as we brought our first lesson to a close. I would open the shutters of the schoolroom and turn off the fan and air conditioning so that we could hear the joyful sound as we worked.

Sundays found us at our church, Juba Riverside Community Church. We met in a long, narrow room at a hotel situated next to the River Nile. The hotel had perhaps seen better days, but it was welcoming. The international congregation came mainly from a host of African nations, but we were a mix of nationalities from all over the world. Our South Sudanese pastor, Bernard, led us with conviction. The two-hour service took some getting used to, though. It was so hot in that room that I often resorted to folding up my printed service sheet and transforming it into a fan, trying to cool the sweat which trickled down my neck. One visiting preacher from Australia commented that he had never preached a sermon in a sauna – until he came to our church!

After the service, we filed outside to congregate around plastic tables and chairs in the shade of magnificent mango trees. Piping hot tea, coffee or hot chocolate was served. Despite feeling utterly overheated at church, the tea was surprisingly reviving. I looked forward to those cups of tea as the hour-long sermon drew to a close.

One Sunday, Ben decided to bring his realistic, black, rubber snake to church. He threw it carelessly up into the branches of a mango tree, then he and his friend, Caleb, waited for it to come back down. Somehow, it managed to come flying back through the leaves to land on the arm of Joel's school teacher. In alarm, Moriah leapt into the air, screaming, 'Snake!' Her hot chocolate tipped over, spilling everywhere. In the chaos, the people sitting nearby scattered in fright. It was a few seconds before Moriah registered that the snake was only a rubber replica. Luckily for Ben, she began to laugh. Gleefully, an unrepentant Ben recounted the story all the way home, a cheeky grin dimpling his face.

There were so many precious moments, treasured friends and unique experiences in South Sudan that I could only look back and marvel. Despite the challenges and despite my misgivings about moving to South Sudan, we never lacked friends nor opportunities. I had been reassured by the promises I read in God's word on our first visit to Juba in 2013. Now I could conclude that the God we followed was indeed a Promise-Keeper.

36

God's protection as gunshots ring out

I opened my eyes. It was still dark. I could hear Andrew moving about the house, getting ready for his day of flying. I had woken earlier than usual and was uncharacteristically alert. Glancing at the bedside clock, I saw that I still had at least forty minutes before needing to meet up with Sue for our 6.40 a.m. jog around the block. The children were not yet up – even my early riser, Ben. These were rare moments of quiet and I grabbed the gift with both hands. I decided to get up, get dressed and use the time to pick up my little book of daily Bible readings. The reading for that day – 28 September 2015 – was Psalm 5. I reached out and opened my Bible.

The words in front of me seemed suddenly magnetic. My book of guided Bible readings suggested that I take careful note of the early verses of the psalm, but instead I found my eyes drawn unintentionally to verses 11 and 12: 'But let all who take refuge in you be glad… Spread your protection over them, that those who love your name may rejoice in you… you surround them with your favour as with a shield.'

Since those words had stood out to me, I decided that I should use them as a prayer for the day ahead, asking for protection to be 'spread over' us, like a blanket; for favour, like 'a shield'. At the same time, I wondered why we might need protection… Was it because there might be danger on my morning jog with Sue?

Over an hour later, I had returned from an uneventful morning run through the streets of an awakening Juba. Smoke was rising from the charcoal fires as chapatti stands prepared for a busy day of trade, shops were opening and people were already milling around the entrance gates of Juba Teaching Hospital. Back at the compound, I sat for a few moments on the wide, stone doorstep of our house, out of breath, allowing the sweat to trickle down my face. I then greeted my three energetic children, now wide awake. Joel came and sat beside me while I mentally listed the tasks ahead before school started at 8.30 a.m. The Bible reading for the day and my heartfelt prayers slipped into the back of my mind as I stood up and pushed open our heavy glass door. It was time to get on with another busy Monday in Juba.

By 3.30 p.m., Esther and Ben had completed their schoolwork and I had walked over to pick up Joel from preschool. At four years old, he now attended JCA School until 3 p.m., which kept him happily occupied while his siblings were busy studying at homeschool. The children asked to go and play with their friends outdoors.

'We might play in the playground, or in Caleb's house,' Ben informed me. He knew that I liked to know where they were, so I could find them easily. Caleb's house was just the opposite side of the playground from our house and schoolroom. Esther, meanwhile, said she would go and visit her little friend, Imani, in the houses belonging to World Relief along the top end of our compound. This gave me a chance to prepare some school lessons and look through Esther's maths, which was becoming more detailed the older she got. So I left the comfort of our cool, spacious lounge and took a bottle of water across to the schoolroom. As the flimsy door of the prefabricated building flopped back into place behind me, I pulled it firmly shut and flicked on the fan to create a breeze.

My mind was engaged with schoolwork, but I was suddenly jolted back into reality with what sounded like a gunshot. Ever alert for this kind of sound in Juba, my head jerked up from the files and lesson plans on the desk. I glanced out of the small window. There was no sign of anyone moving about outside, so maybe I had imagined the noise? It was still worth checking, though. I stood up and took the couple of steps to the door, opened it and looked around outside.

Everything seemed normal. The South Sudanese children in the neighbouring compound, across the roughly woven, wooden fence, were still playing noisily outdoors. I could hear the usual Juba sounds: the building site outside the compound; chickens clucking and scratching around by the fence; traffic in the distance. Nothing different seemed to be happening at the MAF office block adjacent to the schoolroom. I shrugged to myself. It must have been something falling at the building site, I mused, as I turned around and went back to my desk, closing the door behind me.

I had scarcely sat down again when my ears caught another distinct 'bang!' This time, I leapt up. That was definitely a gunshot! Then another. They sounded too close. I flung the door open and was immediately aware of the difference in the atmosphere. There was no noise of children next door – even the chickens were quiet. An eerie silence replaced the sounds of everyday life. I felt myself jump as an even louder gunshot exploded into the tense air, then another. 'Bang! Bang!' There was no doubt that guns were being fired – but where was the shooter? They were obviously nearby, but how close? Were they on our compound? A sickening thought crashed into my mind: *Was the shooter in the playground?*

Suddenly, panic engulfed me as another question rocked me: *Where were my children?* I felt a cold sweat come over me even as I stood in the heat of the open doorway. I didn't know if my boys were in that playground; I didn't know if they were caught up in the firing line; I didn't know if they were terrified, or hurt. Then my knees buckled as confusion took over and an even more horrible question struck my mind: *What if my children had been shot?* That terrifying idea made me shake – I didn't know, in that moment, if my children were still alive… Only yesterday I had spoken with a Burundian church friend who had miraculously survived, a few weeks previously, a shooting incident in his home when thieves broke in. Sadly, his two housemates were shot dead. This was a dreadful reality in Juba. What if this was an armed robbery happening now? Were there merciless gunmen, armed and lethal?

All I wanted right then was to know, urgently, that my three children were safe – but how could I get to them? In those moments of panic, my mind went into overdrive. Questions, scenarios, action plans – thousands of them – seemed to fly in and out of my mind, filling it. I could barely process them. A fuzzy indecision took hold. Should I take a risk and run to the playground? But what if I got shot? I could not help my children if I were injured. I shut the door again and stood, still indecisive, looking through the window as a lone South Sudanese staff member hurried through the MAF car park, crouching, his phone pressed against his ear. My phone! I should phone Caleb's mum!

I picked up my phone, but found it hard to grasp – I realised how much I was shaking. I tried to dial Kristen's number, but my fingers seemed to have turned into jelly. Each time I attempted to pull up her number, my fingers slid off the glassy screen. This simplest of tasks had become a giant challenge for my shaking body. Thankfully, I succeeded and the phone started to ring. To my absolute relief, Kristen answered instantly – and began speaking before I could say a word. Her voice firm and reassuring, she simply stated, 'Liz, your boys are both here with me. They are fine and in the house with me and my kids.' There was a brief pause, then she repeated, 'They are both fine.'

I tried to respond, but discovered it wasn't just my fingers that weren't working. My entire body seemed to be malfunctioning; my voice came out as a choke. I managed a gabbled thanks and felt the tension levels diminish a fraction. Kristen understood. I was so very thankful to hear her words and to picture Ben and Joel in her solid, brick home, with calm, caring Kristen, safe behind locked doors. Now I needed to hear that Esther was fine. I knew she had planned to be inside Imani's house, so she was less likely to be in danger, but of course I wanted to check. As I hung up from Kristen, Imani's mum was already calling me. I answered quickly. It was Esther on the other end of the phone line.

'Mummy, are you OK?' came her unsure, nine-year-old voice. Oh, my sweet-natured Esther. It hadn't yet occurred to me how worried she might be feeling, knowing there were gunshots but not knowing where her mum and brothers were.

I took a deep breath to steady my voice – and it worked. 'Yes, Esther, I am fine. I am inside the schoolroom and your brothers are safely inside Caleb's house.'

Reassured, she explained to me how she and the others in Imani's house were lying on the floor in the lounge, keeping their head down.

My mother's heart ached at this image of my little girl having to lie down on the floor to shelter from the threat of gunfire. It seemed so absurd – and yet it was so real. But how grateful I was that all of the children were safe and with responsible adults. It was also such a relief to hear from other mums that they and their households were fine. I took another deep breath. Standing by the now-locked door, I put down my phone and wondered what to do next. In the last minute, there had been no more gunshots, but we still didn't know what was going on, who was shooting, where they were. How great was the danger? It was that not knowing which heightened the stress of each frightening incident in Juba.

The adrenaline was starting to decrease, but my mind was still buzzing with frightening thoughts like swarms of bothersome insects. Here I was, alone in a room no bigger than a container, cut off from our MAF team and unsure about how to get information on the current crisis. *If we did have armed men of ill intent on the compound, would they think the schoolroom was an office and come here looking for money or computers? If they did, would they see their mistake and leave me alone – or shoot me, like Susan had been shot? Did it hurt to be shot? Would they rape me? Should I try to hide? If so, where?* The children's school desks were too small to crouch under and my desk faced the door, so there was nowhere to conceal myself. My imagination was running away like wild horses. To focus my mind, I even wondered if perhaps I should try to do more schoolwork? That turned out to be a poor idea, since concentration had deserted me.

My phone sprang to life again. I saw Andrew's name flashing on the screen. Phew! He had landed back in Juba. Although I was still shaking, I managed to snatch up my phone and answer quickly. I was disappointed that he was still on the other side of town, but it was wonderful to hear his calm voice. Andrew was concerned. He was not yet allowed to return from the airport until current danger levels were assessed. However, he told me that he had asked a colleague in the office to check on me. He advised me to get to a solid, brick building as soon as possible since, I learnt, the walls of the prefabricated schoolroom are no protection from bullets. I should really lie down on the floor if gunmen were still on the loose, just as Esther was doing.

Before I could take any further action, Stephen, the colleague Andrew had called, arrived from the MAF office to see how I was and to tell me that no sign of any shooter had been detected on our compound. Another huge relief. He advised me to wait for an all-clear text message from manager Bastiaan before I crossed the compound to collect my children, but the short dash to our nearby house should be safe.

As Stephen turned to go, Esther arrived, out of breath. Imani's mum was on her way to the World Relief safe room, but came to me first to deposit my daughter. I hugged Esther close, glad to have her in my arms, and decided that we should move to the security of a solid house. Neither of us wanted to sit in our house alone, so I called my next-door-neighbour, Sue. Fortunately, dexterity had returned to my fingers, so placing that phone call was easy.

'Yes, come over – I'll unlock the door and get the kettle on,' responded Sue, true to her English roots.

Holding hands, my daughter and I dashed across the open space between the schoolroom and our duplex. We were soon sitting comfortably on Sue's sofa with our very British cups of tea. Sue even opened a comforting packet of Bourbon cream biscuits – there is always something calming about chocolate in my opinion. Sitting together in the dim lounge – the curtains were closed to hide us 'just in case', and all the doors were locked – we exchanged stories of where we had been when the shooting began.

The all-clear came soon after, so we thanked Sue and took off, bounding across the compound to collect Ben and Joel. We discovered them playing with a group of children in Kristen's house, diverted and cheerful. They were thankfully none the worse for their short-lived lockdown experience. I thanked Kristen profusely for welcoming the boys, for her sensible response and for keeping the children calm and occupied. I felt my body relax as we set off, all four of us, to return home. As I wandered back through the compound in the early evening light, my three children skipping blithely next to me, I was reassured when we crossed paths with our neighbours, friends and colleagues and personally heard that everyone on the compound was unharmed.

On his return, Andrew found me preparing dinner in our kitchen. He listened to our afternoon's tale, concern etched on his face – and possibly a hint of moisture in his blue eyes. It hit him hard to think of his family being exposed to potential danger, particularly when he was not with us.

The reason for the gunfire emerged that evening: it had been a cruel act of armed robbery. We heard that in the open street that Monday afternoon, three men had been robbed at gunpoint, shot and left for dead. The bright sun, shining overhead in the skies of South Sudan, looked down helplessly on more mindless bloodshed in a country sadly accustomed to violence. Two bodies dropped lifeless on the dusty side street, gunned down near the wooden perimeter of our compound, and one man died later from his wounds. It was horrifying and tragic. Our prayers were with the families concerned.

It was a sobering thought that our children could have been playing by that fence, building their muddy dams in the water outlet that trickled close to the street outside. That fence was certainly not strong enough to block bullets, should they stray from their target.

It was likewise an incredible thought that the boys had decided of their own volition that they wanted that day to play inside – a most unusual decision for these mud-loving lads. Kristen herself told me how astonished she was when a small troop of young boys pushed open her front door and asked to play indoors, shortly before the shots were fired.

Once again, I could not believe that these events and the decision of those little boys were simply coincidence. I had been given that same morning those very specific words to pray. That very afternoon, I witnessed for myself how God spread His protection over us, like a blanket, like a shield.

Gratitude washed over me. The promise I read way back in Tanzania, and which helped us commit to South Sudan, rang true – it was God alone who would keep us safe in a city with too many guns. However, the shock and stress that I had experienced did not just go away – they were to take their toll on my mental health in the months to come.

37

Night invades my mind

Less than two weeks later, our house help Grace arrived for work with her shoulders sagging, her usual smile dulled and her sparkle dimmed. Concerned, I asked her what was wrong. She launched into a disturbing tale of her eighteen-year-old relative who had been killed in Juba on Thursday afternoon.

Grace described how her relative had been drinking tea with a friend when he was caught in the crossfire of a shooting incident that left four people dead, including his twenty-two-year-old friend, a child returning from school and a young lady from Uganda who had been innocently washing her clothes. I agreed at once to Grace leaving work early to go and help her family with funeral preparations. I swallowed my outrage at these lives cut short, but the dangers of gun crime weighed heavily on my mind. If I had not had my children with me in Juba, maybe I would not have felt so anxious. I found myself praying over and over for the safety of our kids.

That same night, I woke at 2.30 a.m. to the sound of gunshots in the distance. I sat up, my heart pounding. Picturing Grace and her family, I sent up a prayer for their protection. A sound that was unsettling before now seemed even more sinister. I wondered who had died, who was hurt. It brought back my own disturbing memories of danger and sent a rush of adrenaline through my body. Juba's shooting incidents were sporadic, but enough to whittle away at my peace and enough to build up an inner tension – though I wasn't yet fully aware of this.

Over six months later, I found that my resilience to bear sad news was wearing thinner. Andrew told me he had heard gunshots one Thursday night, around 2.40 a.m. Later that morning, we heard tragic news. Those gunshots had killed Stephen, our young neighbour, who ran the small shop situated just outside our compound gate, only a stone's throw from our house. Stephen was always pleasant to our children when we popped into the rough wooden structure to purchase phone credit or tea. At other times, I took the children there to practise addition and subtraction skills as they counted out grubby South Sudanese pound notes in exchange for half-melted sweets and chewing gum. I was shaken to realise that an acquaintance of mine had lost his life so violently. I cried for the senseless loss of Stephen's young life. Sadness for his brother, who worked alongside him, and for their family weighed down on me.

Around that same time, Andrew and I were facing pressure to make a decision about the children's education as Esther had only one year left of primary education. On the one hand, I felt duty-bound to stay in South Sudan, which would mean homeschooling at secondary level (a daunting idea) or perhaps a boarding school in Kenya. I knew I could make these options work if I had to; but I didn't like either of them. The other option would be to move to a country where Esther could attend secondary school and still live at home.

I agonised over these choices. We loved working for MAF. It was a privilege to be a tiny part of their work, which brought life and hope and faith into difficult situations. In addition, Andrew loved flying in South Sudan. If God wanted us to continue this work, then who was I to decide otherwise? But I wondered if there was another MAF programme where my growing children could go to secondary school and live with us at home. An unhealthy, dark cloud of guilt started to creep in as I imagined us living in such a place – and I felt like a traitor.

One Sunday morning at church, I was watching my daughter bobbing up and down to the music with her friends. So carefree. So young. As the light caught on her blonde hair, she looked radiant – like the meaning of her name. It caught me unawares and I found tears welling up in my eyes. 'Please don't make me send her away, Lord!' I silently prayed. The next song included the lyrics 'God will make a way, when there seems no other way.' Those words were perfectly timed. I prayed that God really would make a way for us, because I certainly couldn't see one. An internal battle was raging in my heart as I wrestled with the options. Although I prayed, I was forgetting to trust God. I became tearful, tired and fretful.

Tiredness can worsen irritations, making small things feel overwhelming – like the low, mechanical hum of generators near our house, but outside of our compound, which invaded our home and schoolroom twenty-four hours a day. The fact that I could not control the noise level in our home and that I hated the sound wore away a little more of my joy – and my sleep. I stuffed earplugs in at night to deaden the incessant droning. We lined the windows of our bedroom with mattresses to absorb some of the noise, turning our bedroom into a bunker. I laughed with Nadia about the extreme measures I was taking to try to block out a noise she never noticed, despite living next door. It was not a good sign, though. I was moving from living in South Sudan to barely coping with South Sudan. I was heading for burnout.

Being close to burnout meant negativity. My thoughts were turning dark. I made the error of comparing myself to others – the other MAF wives appeared so calm, so in control! In contrast, I looked critically at myself: struggling, indecisive, out of control. There was my indecision about schooling; the guilt about my dreams for our family; a home saturated with noise I could not control; the weight of not being able to turn the tide of poverty I saw in the streets, the cemetery and the hospital; sadness for wasted lives in a city where death arrived with a bang and snuffed out life in an instant; and fears for our safety. My irritability grew, my fuse was short and, despite my dread of conflict, I ended up in a painful clash with another family on our compound. Our conflicting opinions and the resulting strife twisted my stomach and made me feel ill with unease.

One evening, I tried to watch the film *The Good Lie*, which documents the true story of a group of children from South Sudan. The film portrays them running away from violent fighting in their village and walking through inhospitable terrain to reach safety. Their dangerous journey took weeks before they ended up at Kakuma refugee camp in Kenya, a place where Andrew was often flying. Shortly after the film commenced, I burst into tears at the suffering of those children and turned the film off. This was not entertainment – this was real life. Those children could have been a number of people we actually knew in Juba – people who worked alongside Andrew and had spent their childhoods running from the harmful effects of war, losing their families and witnessing unimaginable horrors. I couldn't bear to see their pain portrayed on a big screen. It was too close to home. The trauma of this fractured nation was overwhelming my emotions.

For a short while, I woke early: too early. My eyes flew open, my pulse was racing and my mind felt electrically charged, even though my body felt tired. Glancing at my bedside clock, the red lights blinked indifferently at me in the dark. It was only 3 a.m. – again. Over and over, I woke up at this hour then lay awake in the darkness. I was not accustomed to insomnia. The only other season when I did not sleep well was when I was nursing small children – and then the disturbance came from them, not from me. Why was I so tired, but my mind so alert? Why could I not relax? Occasionally, I got up and went downstairs to make a calming drink of redbush tea – but the insistent generator noise in the kitchen, in the bathroom, in every room irked me and the stress came flooding back. My eyes wet my pillow with silent, night-time tears and my heart cried out to God for a different home – one where there was peace. Peace in the country, peace in the streets, peace in my relationships – and peace without noise in my house.

I tried to be a good missionary wife, to pick up my Bible and to pray. One morning, I came across a verse I had never really noticed before: 'The LORD you God is with you… He will take great delight in you' (Zephaniah 3:17). Instead of finding comfort in these words of affirmation, I found a distasteful cynicism, a kind of swirling darkness, pushing its way into my mind. *Well, there's a verse for* other *missionaries*, I thought, picturing those missionary wives I knew. I imagined God's smile of delight as He assessed their good works and happy obedience while they thrived where God had called them. I put my Bible aside, then made room for Self-Pity, that ugly companion, to speak to me instead: *I bet when God looks at me, He sees a total disappointment, not a delight. Since I can't cope with the calling I was given, I must be a failure. I'm an ungrateful, weak, exhausted missionary wife, who no longer wants to stay in the city where God placed me.*

These negative thoughts weighed me down like a heavy chain. They were still pushing down on me when we set off a few days later for the MAF Day of Prayer, held in a hotel across town. Our family clambered into one of the MAF minibuses to join our entire national and international staff team. I usually loved these special get-togethers – the chance to be with the whole team and have a day off school. However, on that day, I gave up the effort of singing happy songs with energetic, smiling people and of praying with others when such a heavy chain entangled my soul. I had a choice: stay in the meeting and focus on the God who united us, or give in to the dark, oppressive thoughts? I chose the latter. Leaving Andrew and the children with a happy gaggle of MAF kids near the front of the meeting, I slunk away to wallow in my gloom.

Heading down a tiled staircase and around a corner, I entered a large lounge where a giant, wall-mounted TV screen infiltrated the space. The tinny sound of poor-quality speakers blared out today's news. 'Riek Machar is returning to Juba!' shouted the commentator. 'With his own troops!' The frown on my forehead deepened and my heart sank even lower. Would this mean more conflict for war-torn South Sudan? Back in 2013, Riek Machar and Salva Kiir's coalition government had disintegrated, resulting in intense, bloody fighting that claimed many lives. If the two leaders came face to face now, would tensions explode again? My already melancholy mood intensified.

The next day, homeschool resumed as usual – but change was coming.

38

Daylight bursts through the night

It was a new day – another sunny South Sudan day. I took Joel's small hand in mine and we headed companionably across the compound to his preschool. There were now nine students enrolled, which meant it had almost doubled in size since Joel first attended. I briefly greeted the handful of mums at his classroom door, before hurrying back to the schoolroom to begin lessons with Esther and Ben. Finding Esther and Ben seated on the carpet next to the bookshelves, I drew my chair close to start the school day with them.

'Mum,' asked Esther, 'where were you yesterday on the MAF prayer day, at that hotel? I couldn't see you…'

'Yes,' chimed in Ben, 'where did you go?'

'Oh, I'm sorry,' I responded. 'I went downstairs and watched the news.'

'But why did you do that? I was worried!' Esther looked at me, her brows knitted together in a puzzled frown. 'I didn't know where you were, so I thought…' She hesitated. 'I thought, what if you'd been shot?'

'*What?*' I looked at Esther in amazed horror. 'Oh, darling, I'm so sorry – I had no idea you were thinking that! I'm so, so sorry. I should have told you that I was watching the news. Of course I hadn't been shot! There was no danger in that hotel,' I reassured my children. What kind of a job was I doing as a mother, though, if my child's imagination went to the worst, most dramatic scenario? I needed to stop this negativity – and stop letting it infect my family. My children had given me the jolt I needed to refocus.

I tried to encourage my children with some Bible verses about God's protection – but then a thought struck me. I was busy telling them to trust God – but I was worrying so much that I had stopped trusting Him myself. Before I taught trust, I needed to live it. Suddenly, I knew I must make it a priority to carve out time alone with the Lord I professed to trust. I was ashamed of my attitude.

Later, I sought out a quiet place and turned back to Zephaniah 3:17, the verse which I had read with such heaviness a few days earlier. I was afraid to reread it in case the accusation would come at me again that God found nothing delightful when His gaze fell on me. This time, however, something deep had shifted in my heart.

It was like reading the same passage in a different room: one where the blinds had been taken off the windows and sunlight allowed in. The swirling fog of Untruth was dispelled; the sun's rays evaporated the depressive, grey clouds.

'The LORD your God is in your midst', I read once more. I knew He was with me, but wait… I hadn't noticed the next bit of this verse earlier: He is 'a mighty one who will save' (ESV). I stopped right there and was reminded of something crucial. I was saved not because of anything good I did, but simply because God had a plan – *He* sent salvation for me in the shape of Jesus. It was because of *Him* that I was not only acceptable to God, but also delightful. It was because *Jesus* is compassion, kindness, forgiveness and love that He died on that cruel cross to take the punishment for all my ugly deeds and thoughts, failures and weakness. When I accepted this truth many years ago, I had been welcomed into God's family, forgiven, a most dearly loved child. That is why even I could say with conviction, 'He will take great delight in you'.

I read on: 'he will quiet you by his love' (ESV) – wasn't He doing that right now? Calming my fears; reassuring me of His love and acceptance? Reminding me that He is with me in good times *and* hard times, simply because He loves me? The verse continued, He 'will rejoice over you with singing'. God had joy in me as His child because of His character – not because of me. I pieced the fragments of this verse together and saw an amazing truth emerge.

There is nothing I can do to make God love me more – and nothing I can do that makes Him love me less!

If I ever thought that moving to a far-off country in Africa, and working for a missionary organisation like MAF, made Him love me more, then I was wrong. I could not accrue points with God. By the same token, if I got things wrong, if I felt overwhelmed or if I struggled with issues beyond my control, He did not love me less, nor cast me aside as a disappointment. Why? Because of the saving grace of Jesus who stepped into the gap to be the One who is mighty to save. I had missed the key to understanding this verse the first time I read it. God delighted in me because of Him. I was free from trying to earn His love because Jesus had already mightily secured it. I was free from trying to be the perfect missionary wife – there is no such thing. There is only a perfect Jesus, with perfect love for *each* of His children.

Those heavy chains I had been dragging around vanished with a silent puff into thin air, like powdered rust. The pressures, the education question, tricky relationships and the political tensions of Juba had not disappeared – but my attitude changed from that point onwards. I was still tired – but had been given the strength and focus to cool off in God's presence instead of burn out on my own. I again started looking to the God who loved me, confident in His grace and of His presence in all the challenges. I was excited to grasp such a fundamental truth about God's grace – and equally amazed it had taken me so many years as a Christian to understand it.

Suddenly, I realised something else. I had come to South Sudan thinking I could work for God. Instead, I found that God was working in me, helping me to know Him better – and therefore trust Him better.

Just a few weeks later, on our next R and R to Kenya, another pressure was lifted when Andrew and I resolved the education issue. We took the opportunity to visit St Andrew's School in Turi, excited to explore this beautiful, well-renowned boarding school as an option for Esther's and maybe Ben's education and excited to see Andrew's lovely sister again. Yet when I saw my children in the dormitories, it confirmed for me what I already knew deep down: I couldn't bear to part with them – not yet. I wanted to be the one to put them to bed after a day at school and the first one to see them in the morning. I also knew without a doubt that I could not take on the responsibility to homeschool at secondary level. This time, I was free of guilt in our decision, because God had reminded me in His word that I didn't need to try and earn His love by making a decision to stay in South Sudan based on guilt. If we chose to leave South Sudan a few months short of our four-year contract, His nature was grace, and His love would still be with us.

On our return to Juba, Andrew and I walked across the compound to the office of Bastiaan, our manager. We explained regretfully that, while we loved the work of MAF South Sudan, we felt that we could not stay in Juba longer than one more academic year because of our children's educational needs. This gave us just over twelve months in Juba. Once Esther completed her primary education, we would leave. We would be sad to leave the team and the work, but we wanted to pursue the possibility of working for MAF elsewhere. The next step was to pray for God to 'make a way': for MAF South Sudan to have the pilots they need and for our family to remain together elsewhere.

Making a decision was a weight off our minds. For now, we thought, we could relax a little. There was plenty of time ahead before we had to consider the question of what would come after South Sudan. We little suspected how our world was about to change.

39

Danger, as soldiers take to the streets

Friday 8 July 2016 was no ordinary Friday.

The following day, South Sudan was to celebrate five years of independence from Sudan, but tensions were rising. As the TV commentator had promised, Riek Machar had arrived in town with his own troops and been reinstated as Vice President. Rumours abounded. What if the troops loyal to Machar fought against those loyal to President Salva Kiir? What if Independence Day ended up as a day of conflict, with the two factions fighting for control instead of celebrating their nation? There had already been skirmishes across town. My email inbox was flooded with reports of unease and warnings of possible fighting.

Everyone was on edge. The previous morning, I had written in my journal:

Last night, around 8.15 p.m., I listened to 15 minutes of shooting and bangs in the dark. Not sure what is going on – but it is disconcerting. It is the fear of not knowing what is happening coupled with the knowledge of how volatile the situation is... Once it was over, my palms stopped being sweaty and my heart rate calmed down, but while it lasted, my mind raced as fast as my heart, thinking up scenarios of evacuation – what to pack; how to explain it to the children; how we could get to the airport...

Apparently, the shooting sounds I heard were an ammunitions store which had accidentally been set alight. What a relief! But my reaction betrayed the pressure I was feeling as Saturday 9 July drew closer.

Friday 8 July started in the normal way. I was up by 6.15 a.m. and headed to the car park to meet my friend Karyn for our early-morning jog. She greeted me with the disturbing news that five soldiers had died in an incident last night across town – news that the World Relief security staff had passed on just a few minutes earlier. We looked at one another, then debated for a few minutes what we should do. Nobody had told us to stay on the compound.

Just then, I spotted one of our security guards who had recently arrived for his morning shift. We decided to ask him for advice. In his opinion, did the streets feel more dangerous? Would a short run around the block be safe?

He gave us a small smile and said he had not encountered any problems coming to work. We took this as a positive sign – and set off, full of energy, ready to exercise.

It turned out to be the shortest run I have ever done. Within a few metres, it was evident that something was wrong. Maybe it was the uncharacteristic quiet. Maybe it was the strange lack of cars on the streets of our Hai Cinema neighbourhood. Most of all, it was the military vehicle that suddenly stormed past, its open back filled with hard-faced soldiers clutching large guns.

There was no need to articulate how we felt. The tension was palpable. We made a mutual decision that it would be safer to return home, swiftly turned around and headed straight back to our compound. Once we entered the gates, I was consoled to hear the guards secure the gates behind us, locking us into the safety of the MAF compound. Karyn crossed the compound to head home. I was determined to get on with the day as usual for the sake of the children, mentally preparing for homeschool as I walked the few steps home, but at the back of my mind anxious questions were lurking. Would tensions overflow?

That afternoon, I put on a DVD for the children while I sat at my desk in the schoolroom, completing two hours of lesson preparation. I wanted to have the weekend free for time with family and friends. I was also looking forward to dinner that evening. There was no need to cook – we were joining our MAF team and Nathalie's family for pizza at nearby Quality Hotel. Over the course of the afternoon, security situation reports continued to warn us of potential skirmishes, but so far, all was settled in Juba. After a brief debate, the decision was made: it would be safe to go ahead with our early meal out. After all, the hotel was situated so close – just a few minutes' walk away – and we would be safely back before dusk fell at 6.30 p.m.

Therefore, a group of us gathered by the MAF guard house, close to the compound gates, before making our way to Quality Hotel. The children skipped along beside us, carefree at the prospect of a sociable evening together. But within half an hour of arriving, while the children were still deliberating over which flavour drinks they would like, worried frowns started to replace happy smiles.

'Bang!' The first shots were spaced out and the threat was not immediately apparent. Andrew reacted first. He had walked over later than us, after finishing some paperwork. Unnerved by the shots he had heard on his way to the hotel, he wondered if it might be safer to cancel our food order and return to the security of the compound. I was dismissive. This was Juba – the occasional gunshot was not unusual. We turned our attention back to the drinks order.

Suddenly, there was a longer volley of shots. Then another. I tried to ignore the rush of adrenaline, the sense of fear. Perhaps we had deliberated too long. More shots burst into the city air, causing me to jump. This was louder; this was too close; this was dangerous.

Intermittent gunfire followed, then heavier weapons boomed angrily across the city. The hotel locked its doors as we heard the sounds of military vehicles tearing down the road and of people fleeing, the soles of their rubber shoes flapping noisily on the paving.

We started to take action to shield the thirteen children in our party. First of all, a group of us crowded into the bar area, before we realised that its bricks with decorative holes would not protect our little ones from bullets. Stressed and unsure what to do, we tried to squeeze the children into one of the bathrooms. It was too small to contain us. Our desperation to get behind solid walls increased as the gunfire continued. Eventually, one of the hotel staff appeared with a key and fumbled with a lock in a small side door. *That's strange*, I thought. *I've never noticed that door before* – even though we often visited this hotel on Friday evenings. Now we all crowded through its narrow opening and followed the hotel staff into the sheltered inner courtyard to wait out the worst of the shooting. Not knowing what was really going on, how near the gunfire was and how widespread was the fighting, we silently prayed while outwardly reassuring our children with a confidence we didn't feel.

I was amazed at my capacity to stay calm on the outside while inwardly fear was pumping through my body and mind. I jumped with each new burst of gunfire. For the second time in my life – for the second time in Juba – I was terribly afraid. If anyone noticed my trembling legs and my shaking hands, they didn't say so. I thanked God for the long trousers I had worn to ward off mosquitoes because now they provided a useful disguise for my fear.

Over the other side of the yard, I looked at Joel sticking close to his dad. Esther and Ben stayed close to the older children and to me and the other mums. I concentrated hard on keeping calm, on talking to the children or on speaking French with Nathalie.

We glanced at the antics of Ben and Nathalie's son as they skipped from paving stone to paving stone in the space of the courtyard. 'I don't know whether to feel afraid or excited!' declared Ben, honestly. I was glad he was not as shaken as his mother. Being a parent in Juba, responsible for young lives, added a heavy dimension of concern.

We waited, on edge, while our deputy programme manager left to try and get more clarity on the security situation and make plans to get us to safety.

'Will our food come soon?' asked Esther, as she saw one of the waiters hurry across the yard and deliver a boxed pizza to another MAF family. We had paid for our meal, but no longer expected it. We had ordered later than some of the others, just as trouble began and normality ceased. We didn't know when we would eat – or whether we would have to sleep at the hotel. I was thankful we were at least at a hotel with beds, though I wondered vaguely if they had mosquito nets or enough beds. I tried not to picture us stranded at this hotel without solid compound walls.

A period of quiet followed and the shooting became sporadic. We dared to breathe a little more easily. Our deputy programme manager reappeared and gathered us together round one side of the courtyard, the adults and children in a chaotic crowd. We listened gravely to his advice. He explained how the streets nearby seemed calm enough for us to make it back to the MAF compound. To avoid the main road, we must take the back entrance from the hotel. We were to walk in a crocodile formation, in pairs, each child holding hands with an adult. If we heard gunfire, he advised us to lie down on the ground over the children to shield their bodies. Bizarrely, I found myself thinking that I didn't want my children lying on the muddy dirt of Juba's side street because I would never get the dirt out of their clothes, instantly regretting such an inane thought at this critical time.

It felt surreal stepping into the streets of Juba that evening with our colleagues and friends. It was almost dusk, but in the remaining light we traipsed, a bedraggled and solemn procession, back to our compound. Joel clung tightly to Andrew. I walked behind Nathalie and her children, with Esther's hand clasped tightly in my left hand and Ben's in my right. When we reached the junction with the main road, we took a sharp turn to the left to head back down a side street to MAF.

The brief view of the main road sent shivers down my spine. It was lined with soldiers, spaced several feet apart, each holding their gun. Serious, uniformed, alert: they definitely looked ready for combat. The gravity of the situation, our proximity to bloody conflict, struck home. It wasn't worth thinking about what might happen if fighting was triggered again…

I turned at the sound of running feet and spotted a small group of ladies, laden with colourful bundles which they carried deftly on their heads. With their homes situated too close to the fighting, they hastened down our street, seeking shelter.

Being in Juba that night suddenly felt even more menacing.

We walked a few more paces, then finally entered through the tall, metal gates of the MAF compound. As the gates swung shut and the bolts and locks slid into place behind us, we breathed a collective sigh of relief. It felt safer – but still not safe. The threat of danger hung heavily over the city that night.

We were advised to stay safely in our homes, with the doors locked and our outdoor security gates firmly locked too. I turned to Nathalie and invited her and her children to join us behind our locked doors, since none of us had eaten. They were happy to accept and we made our short way across the car park, through the wooden gate and along the concrete path to our house.

Night falls quickly in South Sudan and it was already dark as I headed straight for the kitchen to see what I could rustle up to feed two families. My hands were still shaking as I pulled two bags of pasta and some tins of tuna off the shelf. I discovered some packet-mix sachets for tuna pasta bake that had been sent from England. This was a meal that didn't require much time nor concentration to prepare, which was helpful because both were in short supply that evening. My mind was too distracted to cope with being creative, but being busy cooking helped to calm my shaking.

A quick and easy dinner – this will calm everyone down, I thought.

I was wrong: the meal did just the opposite. As we sat down, a noisy group of nine, the emotions of the afternoon – the tension of the unknown and the fear we had felt – now burst out in an exuberant show of laughter and boisterous games. Now sheltered safely behind solid walls, with the sounds of gunfire fading away, it was like a safety valve had been released. It was a joyful, if hyperactive, evening. Six energetic children ran crazy, up and down the stairs, in and out of the lounge while music belted out all over the house. We laughed, we sang, we enjoyed being together in our home.

It was good that we did. The next day, we were to face decisions which would change our lives and take us away from these and other dear friends. We would never host anyone in our Juba home again.

40

Suspense on Independence Day

Calm finally settled over our home that Friday night. Nathalie and her children, who lived across town, left to stay in a nearby MAF house. Having wrestled three hyperactive children into their beds, Andrew and I found time to talk at last. He was worried. We both were. While we had had released some of the tension at home that evening, we were deeply distressed by the frightening events of the evening. We were starkly aware of how volatile the situation remained.

We sat in our room upstairs, the buzz of the air-conditioning unit ensuring that any wakeful children could not hear our conversation. Andrew confided to me, 'I couldn't tell Joel that everything would be OK, because

I just didn't know what might happen next.' That robbed him of his protective role as father – and hurt.

Andrew wanted to look after us, but these serious events were taking control out of his hands. Stress was creasing his face and dulling the blue of his eyes. This situation was everything we had dreaded about moving to South Sudan: the violence on the streets; the heavy gunfire; the sense of being at the mercy of unpredictable, armed soldiers in a foreign land. We felt vulnerable, afraid and unsure how to protect our children.

We both knew there was only one place we could turn to in this current crisis. Andrew took my hand in his and we bowed our heads. We spent the next minutes praying, asking God for safety, for peace, for divine help in this nation torn apart once again by politics, by violence, by hatred. We understood that even the mindless violence of a potential civil war could not trump the power of our God, who had proven Himself faithful time and again. We asked for wisdom to know what to do and for clear minds to think, even though our bodies felt tired and emotions were still running high.

Sleep was difficult. Andrew managed a few fitful hours, but adrenaline was still coursing through my veins and the fear of renewed gunfire kept me awake. My entire body was on high alert. I lay stiffly on our bed, my ears no longer noticing the generators but straining for the least hint of warning gunfire. I experienced a strange sensation as though needles were spiking my skin, jabbing me all over, all night. It was utterly exhausting.

Over and over, I mentally packed the bag of essential goods we would need to take if we were instructed to evacuate the country. I rose early to start the actual task. I preferred to be doing something, rather than churning events over in my mind and waiting for the next burst of gunfire.

This Saturday 9 July should have been a day of national celebration. Instead, it dawned with an eerie quietness. We were all holding our breath, waiting to see what the repercussions might be of last night's fighting.

Initial news stated that the heavy clashes had left more than one hundred soldiers dead. Online news we read later reported more than 270 deaths, with dead bodies left sprawling on the streets of Juba outside State House. I was haunted by the shocking knowledge that I had heard the deadly sounds which stole those lives. I was horrified that my children had been exposed to such a terrible, frightening noise.

A few weeks later, I watched a news report from Juba which showed the bullet holes and the damage to State House. I felt sick as I glanced at the screen – but broke down in tears as the camera angle moved to show blood on the street being hosed away by strong jets of water. Though diluted, the water could not disguise the deep-red colour of life as it spread over the surface of the road – the very road we used to drive to the supermarket. It was strange to see that juxtaposition between such normal, everyday tasks and instant death – right there on the same street. I once more felt a deep grief for the waste of life and a horror for the bloodshed on streets not far from our home. I continued to carry the shock that my children had been in a place where danger had taken a step too close to our family, our MAF team, our friends.

Back in Juba that Saturday, Independence Day, the children woke full of energy, despite the unusual events of the previous day. Since it wasn't a school day, Esther, Ben and Joel ate their Weetabix for breakfast then burst through our front door and into the compound, full of life and happy to greet playmates for a new day of fun and games. I was pleased they would get some time with their friends, trying not to think about their grief if we had to leave these playmates suddenly. I knew from our time in Nairobi how the grief of leaving their home and the country where they lived could seriously affect the children.

I was distracted as I cleared away the dishes and carried them through to the kitchen to wash with last night's still dirty dishes. The weather was already warm, so I opened the glass window to let in some air and rolled the fly screen into place to prevent insects entering our home. After filling the washing-up bowl with warm water and soapy bubbles, I stood by the sink in front of the window to start washing up. It then started to dawn on me that something felt different. What was it? Abruptly, the silence hit me.

The absence of noise on that Saturday morning was overwhelming. In a flash, I recalled the tense moments of that September day when three men were shot in the street, when local life stilled. Today was just the same.

There were no voices, no sounds of traffic or cooking on charcoal stoves, no children shouting over the wall next door, not even the squawk of a chicken. It was the kind of silence that signalled collective fear. It was uncanny. It was unsettling. Everyone was hiding. The people were afraid. Suspense was in the air – and it invaded my home.

The unease added a frantic tension to my busy morning and I rushed about in a stress-fuelled frenzy. I was grateful for the action – it kept my mind off the uncertainty – but it contorted my stomach into knots. Dashing all over the house, I located important documents and chargers for our phones and laptop, and packed items from our list of evacuation necessities. I searched for our paracetamol and found toothbrushes, shoes suitable for running, enough clothes for each of us to last two days and, of course, the children's teddies – remembering the significance they played in previous transitions. I placed the teddies near, and not inside, our evacuation bag. There they sat, these three comforting reminders of home. If we had to leave, the children might prefer to carry them in their arms.

I counted out wages for Grace to collect and rushed across the compound to leave them, and our spare house keys, with those people who had to stay. I invited them to use any food in our house if we left. If things got worse, the shops would be shut – and it would not be safe enough to go off the compound anyway.

Meanwhile, Andrew faced one of the most difficult mornings of his life. He joined senior staff and the pilots in a series of meetings to review the security situation and make the final decision on whether evacuation was necessary. What a weight of responsibility to make such a significant decision. It was tough for the whole team. How do you predict the future? How do you know whether the current lack of gunfire meant an end to hostilities, or the calm before a mighty storm of destruction?

The staff had a series of security manuals to consult, but did what was right by praying together. They asked for the very best kind of wisdom – God's – to guide their decision-making. Even so, it took a morning of discussion and of reviewing news reports, security reports and manuals. Mixed messages filtered through about road blocks springing up in town and general unrest. One thing was sure: the airport was closed. If MAF did decide to evacuate from Juba, it would be necessary to secure permission from the authorities. That added an extra layer of stress.

If we did evacuate, non-essential staff, women and children would be flown out by two pilots. Essential staff would remain, which meant another pilot must remain in Juba to fly them out later if the security situation deteriorated further. But how do you decide which pilots should stay and which ones could leave with their family? It was a decision loaded with emotion.

Hearing Andrew came home mid-morning, I rushed to the hallway to ask if a decision had been reached. 'Not yet,' came the reply. My dear husband looked tired and the frown on his forehead showed the weight of the impending decision. The suspense was keeping us all on edge. Andrew walked over to his desk to gather a few papers, then disappeared back to the MAF office.

Thankful that at least I had a little more time to prepare for departure, I decided to turn off all the electric sockets. As I hurriedly pulled out the plugs in the lounge, I glimpsed our photo albums. All our precious family records were in these heavy books and I wished I could pack them, but we had a strict allocation of three bags and a limited weight allowance in the event of our evacuation. A sense of loss worked its way into my heart.

I slipped out to our schoolroom to pack some schoolwork. Pushing the key into the lock was a daily, mechanical task, but today felt so different. Would my children study here again? This room held a wealth of schoolwork – two years of achievement and progress. How sad to leave it unfinished. My eyes happened upon the files neatly organised on my desk. All that preparation I had completed yesterday afternoon proved to be a waste of time! I could not carry all the resources to teach those lessons. In fact, I could take very little indeed. Suddenly, tears threatened. I didn't want to leave like this, interrupting my children's schooling and rushing away from their beautiful art and clever work. As I locked the door on my way out, I prayed for protection over our little school and that nothing would be destroyed if looting began in Juba.

Returning home, my phone began to ring. It was an upsetting call with one of the pilot wives. None of us wanted our husbands to stay behind – but one of us would have to face that reality. We were both distraught at the prospect. As I tried to comfort her, I felt a leaden weight settle on me too. If Andrew flew us out of Juba and my friend's husband stayed behind in what could erupt into a war zone, how awful I would feel. How would they make the decision? The knots in my stomach tightened.

I walked over to the office block to drop something off and found Andrew having this very same conversation with Eivind, his fellow pilot and my friend's husband. Looking serious, they stood facing each other in the small space between the kitchen area and the operations room.

'Liz, would you mind if I stay in Juba?' asked Andrew. I was torn between wanting him with us in the plane and wanting my friend to have her husband with her.

'I don't know... I don't mind who decides to stay or go,' I answered, wanting to pass off the responsibility for such an emotive decision. I tried to smile – but there was nothing happy about such an outcome.

It was still only a theoretical question at this point – our departure was not yet confirmed. The two men continued to look at one another, both wanting to do the right thing – by their wives, by their families, by MAF, by each other. They shared a mutual respect and their friendship went back several years. It was a heart-stopping moment.

Then Andrew took a deep breath and spoke up. 'Actually, if I am honest, I would prefer to fly...' His voice took on a strange, anxious quality. 'I need to see my family safe... I need to see Joel safe.'

His words tailed way. I knew that reassuring Joel after the uncertainty last night was high on Andrew's priority list.

Eivind jumped in at once. He knew how disturbing yesterday's evening at Quality Hotel had been for our family and we were all grateful that his children had not been with us last night. 'Of course, of course… we can make it work.'

Eivind graciously conceded so that Andrew could fly us out of Juba. The respect I feel for him will always remain. This was God's kindness in action. This was grace.

I left the men to return to their meetings and discussions, which were taking a stressful toll on the team. I sent up a quick prayer of thanks that Andrew could accompany us if we left and another prayer for wisdom.

Walking back into the compound, I paid a quick visit to friends and to wish them well, just in case we left. When I saw Nathalie, I decided to pass her my prized round of cheese (a luxury in Juba). 'If we don't leave, you need to give it back!' I quipped with a smile, although the thought of leaving her and her family behind in Juba was already making me sad. As YWAM staff, they would not be able to evacuate with us.

We were still in a state of suspense – but at least there had been no gunfire today. I briefly stopped to check on the children in the playground. They were hot and sweaty from their active games in the midday heat and still in blissful ignorance. I left them to enjoy their friends. *It might be the last time they play together in this playground,* I thought, a strange sadness grasping at my heart as I rushed back to our house.

I hurried through to the kitchen to see if I could find something quick for our lunch – although I had barely been able to eat all morning. My stomach was still churning too much to contemplate food. Just then, the sound of the front door announced Andrew's return from his long morning of meetings. I stepped into the hallway to see if there was a decision. I was taken aback to see Andrew just standing in the middle of the hall, ashen faced.

'We're leaving,' he said. Then he suddenly started to cry.

My husband, my pillar of strength, was crying. I had never seen him this broken. It was too much for him: hearing the gunfight; not knowing what was happening; not feeling able to protect his family, his children; the stress; the pressure of decisions which affected our whole community.

However, there was no time to decompress. Now Andrew had to rally himself to prepare for the flight out of Juba, in the context of civil unrest. The stress was far from over.

I rushed to his side. I had nothing to say. So this was it. We were evacuating our home.

41
Escape from Juba

The land cruiser, this hot body of metal under an even hotter sun, felt suffocating as it made its way out of the car park. It turned sharply to the right, taking us away from our home – perhaps forever. I grabbed hold of the seat as we bumped over the hard mud and up out of the potholes. There was the soft sound of crying next to me as one of the women grieved those we were leaving behind.

'Mum, look, there's a soldier lying down with his gun!' Eight-year-old Ben leaned across the car to get my attention. 'Why is he hiding?' he added.

'Don't point, Ben,' I chided him, anxious not to draw any more attention to our party. We were already too obvious: two vehicles advancing down the otherwise deserted streets towards Juba airport. Anyway, I couldn't turn my head to see where Ben was gesturing. I was jammed between perspiring bodies and the bursting suitcases that had been hurriedly tossed in as the pressure to leave mounted.

The younger children, sitting up near the driver, started a game. I was thankful that they had not grasped the danger, but their resilience created a sharp contrast with my own tension.

The vehicle slowed. Oh no, a checkpoint! I strained to see what was happening out of the front windscreen. A couple of soldiers in uniform... My palms were already sweaty but now the thumping of my heart felt audible. Could the others hear it pounding over the roar of the engine? The driver wound down his window, while one of our local staff began negotiating with the armed soldiers. Those guns – I hated the sight of them; I hated how they could take a life. I had heard enough of that last night.

Waiting was agonising. Would they wave us through to the airport? Or would the situation turn nasty? There was no way of predicting the reaction of these military men. We were in their hands – or were we? I breathed another quick prayer, 'Oh God, please keep us safe!' – for what felt like the thousandth time.

God heard our prayers. A few minutes later, one of the soldiers waved us through, unsmiling. Our wheels started rolling and within minutes we were parking in front of Juba's strangely deserted airport. Tense, our two car-loads of parents and children tumbled out of the land cruisers, torn between an urgency to get from danger to safety and the shock of leaving our homes so suddenly. Too suddenly.

We passed in a blur through the unusually quiet airport. The contrast with normality hit me hard. Juba International Airport stood still. Gone was the normal crush of noise, colour and heaving, sweaty passengers.

We were on the tarmac of the airport. Andrew's shirt was already dripping from the heat and the effort of preparing the MAF plane for our evacuation. Two of our South Sudanese staff rushed around the aeroplane, assisting Andrew and Eivind, who had kindly accompanied us to the airport. Our three bags sat on the baking ground, waiting to be stashed in the hold. The forceful afternoon sun bore down on us, its intensity exacerbating the compulsion to get away. To get away from the heat, to get away from the trouble.

Not everyone felt like I did, though. 'But *why* do we have to go?' erupted a distressed Esther, pacing the tarmac, squeezing her teddy harder. As predicted, her faithful teddy was in her arms as a comforter. Tears of frustration shimmered in her blue eyes. 'It's not fair! I want to go *home*! I want to be with my friends!'

'I'm so sorry, Esther.' I wished I could make it better for my children. I wished I could take them safely home. But today, safety meant leaving our home – as quickly as possible.

I glanced at the waiting plane. Preparations were taking longer than expected. Andrew looked concerned.

'Is something wrong?' I enquired, dreading an affirmative answer.

He gave me a stressed glance. 'Just a warning light that shouldn't be on...' His voice tailed off as Eivind leapt into the cockpit to help with troubleshooting.

My stress levels rose even higher. Did this mean we had a technical fault? Would we be forced to turn around and risk driving back through a volatile Juba to our compound? I didn't know if I had the strength to face another nerve-wracking drive with our children through this city in conflict. Or another night on edge, my body taut, praying danger away.

Just then, Ben yelled and pointed at the other MAF plane. It was lining up for take-off. What an incongruous sight this lone aircraft was on a normally hectic runway. I could barely watch as the other MAF plane sped up and started its ascent, carrying three other MAF families to safety. Relief for them merged with a strange sense of abandonment. I swallowed hard to hide my heightened fear for our family and the lone British passenger joining our plane. The authorities had granted us only a limited amount of time to fly out of their airport. If our plane could not fly... I could not bear to imagine the possible consequences.

The roar of the other plane's engine faded into the blue skies, replaced by the sound of young voices as my boys played, like jungle explorers, at the edge of the tall, swaying grass which separated the apron from the runway. I was grateful to see them distracted despite the tension.

All of a sudden, I registered another, most welcome, sound: 'The plane is ready – it's time to board!' came Andrew's voice. A wave of relief flooded my tired body with the realisation that there was no technical fault to prevent our flight. Andrew and Eivind, following a series of checks and hurried phone conversations with MAF engineers in Nairobi, had concluded that our plane was fully airworthy. We said a hurried goodbye to Eivind, our friend who had agreed to remain in Juba and allow Andrew to fly out. His selfless act meant the world to us. As I thanked him, I wished I had the right words to convey this.

I grabbed Joel's hand, helping my small, five-year-old son navigate the steep metal steps up to the cabin of the plane. I checked that Esther was close and was relieved to note that the other passenger was climbing up quickly behind us. Ben joined his dad in the cockpit – a special concession for this unusual flight.

The propeller started to whirr. The mechanical sound of the engine drowned out my final instructions to the children to keep their seatbelts fastened. Andrew, headphones in place, turned and looked at me – his expression reflecting the utter relief I felt. This was it – no going back now.

Slowly, then gaining speed, the plane zipped down the runway. Its nose pointed upwards as we started to rise above the country we had called home for two years. A lump formed in my throat when I looked down at Juba's airport and saw the solitary figure of our South Sudanese colleague, who had helped prepare our plane. He was dancing a jig of farewell. My heart was torn – he was helping us foreigners escape a danger which still raged around him and his family on the ground. Why should we get away from the danger while colleagues and friends were left behind? Guilt mingled with the relief, chewing up my insides, and I was anxious about the safety of those we left behind. If only we could gather up all those we loved in this land and take them with us.

Soon, the airport was just a distant, grey strip, the River Nile was already disappearing under the wings of the plane and we were slipping over the greenery of South Sudan. I suddenly had nothing more to do except sit back while Andrew flew us into northern Kenya. The shock began to set in. I sat rigid in that aeroplane seat, an exhausted Joel slumping down next to me, his head on my knee and his eyes closing in sleep. Gently stroking his blond hair, I thanked God for the safety of my family in that aeroplane. I love MAF flights, I love the incredible views from their small aircraft windows, but today I saw nothing of the vast land stretched beneath us. My restless mind also filtered through the faces of those still surrounded by hostility. 'O Lord, please, *please* take care of those left in Juba tonight. Please keep them safe.' The petition became a repetitive reel, whirling over and over until, finally, my husband's voice cut in on the plane's intercom. We were flying over Kenya's Lokichoggio, our destination. It was time to descend.

The brown earth was drawing closer. The rough structures of this remote town loomed larger as the plane dropped lower for its final approach into the small airport. I stared out of the aeroplane window at the spindly, brown bushes, the dusty streets, the lone cyclist heading slowly into town, the goats bent on grazing. It looked so calm, so unchanged. There were no booming echoes of gunfire here – just peace. As the plane's altitude fell, it was matched by a small decrease in my tension level.

The wheels of the plane touched down. We came smoothly to a stop. The click of seatbelts unbuckling and the sound of the door handle being jerked downwards punctuated the tranquil silence of Lokichoggio. It was time to alight from this plane which had carried us to safety. The children clambered down, teddies tucked under their arms, chattering, hungry and already curious about this next stage of our journey. It was too late to continue to Nairobi as the other MAF plane had done, so tonight we would sleep in a guesthouse close to the airport. I followed them down the steps and stepped out on to Kenyan ground, smiling gratefully at Andrew. We had made it! I knew that was largely thanks to my dedicated husband, who had flown us out of Juba under intense pressure.

Andrew was still on duty, preparing the plane for its overnight stop here in Lokichoggio and distracted by the responsibility to get us to Nairobi tomorrow. The worry on his face had eased a little, though. I could see how reassured he felt as a fellow MAF pilot – Mark from South

Africa – strode across the apron, hand outstretched to greet him and with kindness written all over his face. He had based himself in Lokichoggio for the specific purpose of helping in the South Sudan crisis. We were so grateful for his practical support.

So here we were in Kenya. Here we were in safety! I was thankful – yet still stunned. There would be difficult moments ahead, but for now I focused on the job in front of me: our three children. I turned and stepped purposefully towards the guest house which consisted of little thatched huts. It was time to get these little ones washed, fed and to bed. Tomorrow would be another step on our journey out of Juba and onwards to Nairobi.

42

Evacuation to Kenya

Esther was indignant. 'I'm not sleeping in this bed! Not with *that!*'

I had to laugh – it was a pleasant reprieve from the tension. In the bed we would be sharing that night, Esther had drawn back the sheet to discover a long, filthy toenail. Since it did not belong to either of us, we could only conclude that the sheets had not been changed since the previous guest. I was too tired to care, but Esther was clearly repulsed. I rearranged the bed, moving her pillow across to the other side. We had to sleep top to tail with the hardest pillows. It was eleven o'clock before Esther was able to relax enough to sleep. I wasn't sure how much of her stress was due to the dirty toenail or the pressure of leaving our home so suddenly. I secretly thought that the offending toenail gave my daughter a helpful distraction from the sadness of leaving her friends in Juba.

It took me even longer to sleep. I was still on edge. I wondered how the boys were getting on in an adjacent hut. It was a fitful night, my mind running over the events of the previous hours. My dreams were confused and I woke frequently. When the monkeys in the treetops outside began their noisy morning chatter, I was glad to throw off the sheets and get busy with preparations to move on to Nairobi. Keeping occupied was so much better than having time to think.

Andrew greeted us at breakfast with bleary eyes. Sharing a bed with his two sons and particularly sharing one of the hard pillows with Joel had not been conducive to sleep. In any case, his mind was active, mentally preparing for our onward flight. It would be a while before Andrew had time to process the traumatic scenario from Quality Hotel and the upsetting lack of control he had felt.

Soon, we made our way back across the road to the small airport. It was even quieter than usual since it was Sunday morning with few flights. Waiting for a MAF flight on a Sunday morning, when MAF usually rested, felt strange. It reminded me of the urgency of our situation. The plane we arrived in last night had left, with Mark at the controls, earlier that morning to fetch a family who worked for a different mission organisation just across the South Sudan border. When the plane returned to Lokichoggio, we would climb aboard and Andrew would take over as pilot, evacuating all of us to Nairobi. Andrew was busy, preoccupied with his flight duties and preparation.

I sat on a hard, metal chair in the breezy waiting area, watching the children collect bugs and caterpillars. Ben had carried some plastic friends out of Juba in his pocket: a snake and a scorpion. I heard shouts of dismay from the Kenyan staff as they spotted the scorpion on a luggage trolley. Alarmed, one of them leapt dramatically into the air! A delighted Ben leapt forward to grab it bravely. There were shouts of laughter when the staff realised the joke. Ben was lucky that the airport workers were so good-natured. I was comforted by their kindness to my children.

While waiting, I checked the news – and was shocked. Fighting had resumed early this morning – but of an even higher intensity. Gunfire and heavy weapons boomed destructively throughout the city. Many more lives would be counted among the death toll that day. Hearing my phone buzz, I picked it up to have a disturbing phone conversation with a British friend still in Juba. I walked out of the waiting area and stood in the gentle morning sun at the edge of the airstrip while listening to my distraught friend. I was holding my phone close to my ear so that the children could not overhear.

As we spoke, I could hear muffled bangs in the background. 'Can you hear them?' she shouted. 'Can you hear? It's gone crazy!'

My friend described the sounds of artillery that she and her family were forced to listen to and how she was hiding in the bathroom, her children with her, terrified. I could picture the upsetting scene and the fear for her children was tangible – a fear with which I could identify. My legs felt unsteady again.

She asked if I knew whether MAF could fly them out and I advised her to call the office, but I didn't think any flights would be able to leave that day. The airport was shut and no flight permissions were being granted. When we hung up, I was brushing away tears of both compassion and frustration that there was nothing I could do to help my friend and her family get out of a city in turmoil. She was afraid – and I was helpless. Guilt for leaving when we did came flooding back, along with the conflicting sense of gratitude that we got out when we did. If we had waited, what would my children be doing in Juba today? To what would they be listening?

As I looked at my emails, the news got worse. The situation reports from Juba described impromptu roadblocks, acts of aggression and increased shooting. It was even more difficult to cross town. I wondered how Grace, my house lady, was doing, but phone lines were scrambled. It was surprising that my friend had managed that earlier phone call to me. All of a sudden, a new email flicked across my screen. It was very bad news. Friends we had left behind in Juba had been caught up in an act of violence. I scanned the email – and felt sick. Goosebumps covered my body and I put my head down between my knees to recover my thoughts. My body heaved, but thankfully I didn't vomit. I sat up and looked around. I wondered whether Andrew had read the email? One thing was for sure: the children must not know. Suddenly, the email disappeared, seemingly because it was too upsetting for general distribution and had been recalled. I could see why. Thankfully, I had read enough to know that our friends had since reached safety. For this, I was grateful.

When we eventually boarded the MAF plane, it was a subdued flight. Even the children were quiet as we flew over the picturesque, green hills bordering the Great Rift Valley. Reality was settling in. Questions were starting to surface. How long would we be in Kenya? Where would we stay? How were our friends and colleagues in Juba getting on? Were they safe? Would the conflict get worse, or would the fighting settle down? When could we return home? They were exhausting questions to consider, especially when we didn't have the answers.

Our most urgent question of accommodation was soon answered, though. As we landed at Nairobi's Wilson Airport, we were consoled by the presence of Steve, the MAF Kenya programme manager, who welcomed us with kind concern. We appreciated him giving up his Sunday afternoon to come and meet us. He told us we would stay in the home of generous friends on the MAF compound in Nairobi's Kilimani neighbourhood, since they were currently away overseas on home assignment.

Nor did the kindness stop there. When we reached their house, we were comforted by a welcome basket of tasty food, a card filled with kind words, beds that had been made and fresh towels laid out for us. Steve's wife, Katie, was waiting at the door to welcome us and the kettle was already boiled. I gratefully accepted her hug, the cup of tea and the compassion. What a caring organisation we worked for, where staff acted with tender-hearted thoughtfulness, putting God's love into action for us harried evacuees.

That night, as we sat in the peaceful home on this leafy, spacious MAF compound, we thanked God for our safety. We thanked Him for kind friends, for His goodness and for His protection. He had given us the incredible opening to fly out of South Sudan even when the airport was closed. We prayed fervently for those still in Juba, for calm, for protection, for provision. We mentioned our friends by name and asked God to make a way to get each of them to safety.

We prayed again for peace in South Sudan, where the hatred of a minority made life so hard for the majority. The South Sudanese we knew were people like us – people who wanted to live in peace, raise their families, feed their children and have access to education. We were seeing first-hand how war struck fear, disruption and havoc into the lives of those caught up in its dark, tangled web. Yet we were viewing it now from a place of safety, while for so many the nightmare was an ongoing reality – and this fact haunted my dreams.

I woke up at night, sweating, gasping for air. I leapt out of bed to check on my children. My dreams tried to make sense of the fear I felt in Juba. Nightmares pressed down on me in which I was trying to find Esther, to hide her from the soldiers in uniform. Another distressing night took me back into Juba. I had Esther in one hand, Ben in the other, but I couldn't find Joel. I was running past Quality Hotel, past Landmark Hotel, then found myself outside State House, then on the road to Juba airport. Hordes of refugees surrounded me, with bundles balanced on their heads, a surge of anxious people trying to get out of Juba while gunfire crackled in the distance. I couldn't leave, though. I had to find Joel!

I woke again and sat up, hyperventilating. I took some deep breaths to calm down. Joel was crying. I got up and went to him, then picked him up, grateful that we were together. He too was distressed and unsettled. His life had suddenly changed and he was sensitive to the stress Andrew and I were feeling. Since trying to coax him back to sleep seemed pointless, we went through to the kitchen to make a warm drink. The two of us sat in companionable silence, the dim light of the kitchen casting a gentle glow on our midnight meeting. Outside, the quiet night felt friendly, non-threatening. It felt so good to be safe!

In the morning, I tried, successfully this time, to phone Grace. She and her two children had run to the UN camp in town when gunfire broke out, but in her panic, she had tripped and hurt her ankle. Her family also needed money for food and water. I told her about the wages waiting for her on the MAF Juba compound – but it was still too dangerous to cross town. She would collect it when she could. I was concerned too for the unborn baby she was carrying, but she reassured me that her pregnancy was going well, despite everything. I was relieved to hear that and to know that she had taken shelter.

Monday was another day of heavy fighting. The news coming out of Juba upset us all. We took comfort from the fact that our MAF Juba team was together in Nairobi. I spent much time with Nadia, which helped us both, her friendship lending me strength in the crisis.

That night, we welcomed the news that a ceasefire had been declared in Juba. If hostilities really stopped, our South Sudanese friends could return to their homes, cross town and eventually get on with their lives. In addition, more of our team could fly safely out of Juba on the remaining aircraft and wait in Kenya until the situation stabilised. Hopefully, other airlines would get permission to fly into Juba again and so could bring our non-MAF friends out of a city that had become so menacing.

Over the remainder of that week, we celebrated each time another group came safely out of Juba. More, but not all, arrived from our MAF team, as well as from World Relief, Samaritan's Purse, Tear Fund... Our friends working for these and other organisations were safe. It was one thing to hear that our friends were safe, it was even better to speak to them on the phone, but there was something powerful in actually seeing each other again, face to face – like the comforting warmth of sunshine replacing stormy skies. We made it a priority to meet and sat in the cafés of Nairobi, sharing our stories, glad to be together in a safe place.

It was sad that we didn't get to see Nathalie and her children, but we were glad to hear that they had successfully evacuated to Uganda. I was incredibly relieved to see my

British friend that I had spoken to from Lokichoggio airport. I threw my arms around her and instantly noted how shaken and pale she was. Her concerned husband told me she had been unable to speak for days. The shock of this latest conflict in Juba had taken its toll.

We all needed time to process and get over the shock of these sudden events, of exposure to the sounds of killing, of fear for our children's safety. We needed to come to terms with evacuating our homes. It had impacted us all.

43
A sign of God's goodness

For months, Ben had been complaining of a 'stinging' pain in his stomach. Often, it was accompanied by short bouts of diarrhoea. Sometimes, it caused him to feel sick and lose his appetite. While still living in Juba, he would sit in the lounge pale and listless, stripped of his usual bubbly, bright enthusiasm for life. Then, a few days later, he would bounce back to being Ben – before the strange stomach pain recurred.

We tried eliminating gluten from his diet. We tried cutting back on dairy products. Neither made any difference. We started to put it all down to too much exposure to mud. When your son is drawn like a magnet to mud, we reasoned, it is no wonder he picks up weird bugs. Ben spent hours of his Juba life building dams in muddy water, in the humid climate where bacteria breed fast and furious.

A few days after evacuating from Juba, Ben's stomach pains started again. This time, however, they seemed worse. We took him to see a doctor who was trained in tropical diseases, conscious that this was a privilege that we did not have access to in Juba. We hoped to get answers, but examination of stool samples could not enlighten the medical team. On Saturday, six days after our evacuation, he started to feel even worse. He stayed indoors and we kept him close to the toilet for the frequent, necessary visits. By Sunday afternoon, Ben was in a state. We tried to keep him hydrated as the vomiting began to take even more energy from his body. We tucked him up in bed, where he lay fretful and unhappy, his blond hair sticking out from under the covers.

'I wish I could take his temperature,' I complained to Andrew later that evening, but our thermometer was at home in Juba along with my usual first aid kit. Ben didn't feel hot to my touch, even though he was starting to act like he had a high temperature, shivering and pulling the blankets closer. Every time I gave him a drink, he would vomit out the liquid. When he needed the bathroom, his legs refused to work and he could no longer stand, so I had to carry him. I had nursed my children through many similar illness in East Africa, but not with this strange stomach pain and weak legs that wouldn't take any weight.

'Let's call the doctor again,' suggested Andrew. He made the call, but the surgery was closed this late on a Sunday evening and the now off-duty doctor advised us to bring him in tomorrow morning. Ben started to gabble odd words, disturbed and half asleep. I sat by his bed in the darkened bedroom, stroking back the sticky hair from his forehead and encouraging him to take sips of water from the cup next to his bed. He then became semi-conscious and delirious. A model railway set ran across the bedroom where Ben was staying. As I leaned in towards him, I could just about make out the words he was mumbling: 'Stop the train!'

Then he started to get worked up and thrashed around in his bed, his eyes still closed. 'Get the soldiers away!' he shouted. 'They're coming to get me! Stop! Stop it!'

Concerned, I tried to soothe my eight-year-old. 'It's OK, Ben, there are no soldiers here! And the train is just a toy. You're safe... you're fine...'

It seemed his subconscious was revealing a hidden fear. I wondered whether it was linked to the hostile sights Ben had witnessed on our stressful drive through Juba just over a week ago. When we reached Nairobi, Ben had drawn a picture of the soldiers he saw lying behind the wall, guns poised for action. It was a sinister sight; perhaps my boy was more worried than he had been able to express.

Upset for him, I prayed, 'O Lord, please give my boy peace! Please make him better!' I had my Bible nearby and I reached for it. This was one item that I knew I must throw into our suitcase as I packed up our home. Apparently randomly, my Bible fell open at Psalm 86: 'a band of ruthless men seeks my life, and they do not set you before them' (verse 14, ESV). Thankfully, nobody was seeking to take our lives right now, but Ben was feeling under threat. He was worrying about soldiers, about guns. He had heard men killing one another – ruthless men, without regard for life. This threat had felt very real to me, too, as we stood outdoors at Quality Hotel. It seemed so apt that I should find this psalm right now.

'But you, O Lord, are a God merciful and gracious … Turn to me and be gracious to me; give your strength to your servant' (verses 15–16 ESV). 'Yes, Lord! Ben needs strength, please can you restore it?' I asked. The next part of verse 16 made me sit up straighter: 'save the son of your maidservant' (ESV). We were all called to be servants of the Lord, so as His maidservant, I too could pray these words over Ben: 'Please, God, save my son! Please give him peace, please stop this sickness.' I read the final verse and adapted it to continue my prayer for Ben: 'Please do what this psalm says and "give me a sign of your goodness", so that others can see that you have "helped" us and "comforted me"!'

The sign came sooner rather than later. Ben stopped his struggling, his fretting and his mumbling. He rolled over, drifting into a blissfully peaceful sleep. There was no more rushing to the loo. No more vomiting. No sign of fever now. When daylight came, I crept in and found him grinning cheekily and looking well rested. His stomach was settled too. Ben was back! I smiled at him and ruffled his hair. It was time to make him some breakfast.

I rushed to tell Andrew on my way to the kitchen. We looked at each other, delighted and amazed. Last night, a phone call with my parents informed us that St John's

Church in Burscough, Lancashire had stopped their service to pray specifically for Ben. Shortly after their prayer time, I saw for myself peace settle over Ben – and in the morning, I saw how healing had settled over his body. I had asked God for a sign of His goodness, and He had given it to me.

Despite all the confusion and chaos of the past week, and despite living out of suitcases in a home belonging to another family while grieving the home we left behind, God had not forgotten us. He reminded me of His kindness and compassion. He comforted me with a reminder that His presence is always with His people and that His love can be shown through people far away. He answers the prayers of His people, whether they are praying in England for a small boy in a distant land, or for their son taking refuge in a Kenyan house that doesn't belong to them.

This sign of God's goodness gave me strength and boosted my confidence as we moved from Nairobi to England for our home assignment. We still had so many unanswered questions ahead of us – but we also had a loving God who was faithfully going before us.

44

Back to England – and into the unknown

Travelling to England for the summer months was convenient timing. We could not stay indefinitely in our friends' home in Nairobi. The future was uncertain. South Sudan was uncertain. Taking a flight to England at the end of July gave us two months of reprieve.

England soothed our tired minds and gave us time to recuperate. The love and care of family and friends both comforted and restored us. We visited several churches, giving many talks about MAF's work in South Sudan, about our experiences and about God's recent protection at a time of great need. People were welcoming, interested and kind.

However, my heart was yearning for Africa. I still grieved the sudden loss of our home and the scattering of our community. I wondered where and how our church friends were – we had not heard from many of them since the fighting erupted. I was anxious when I heard news reports about South Sudan and prayed passionately for peace to be restored to a land that had worked its way into our hearts. I worried about Grace and I wondered how our national staff were coping with the ongoing disruption that sporadic outbreaks of fighting were causing all over the country. Hearing that MAF were able to make some flights in and out of South Sudan, I worried for the safety of our pilots. At the same time, I found it difficult to speak of what had happened at Quality Hotel and our evacuation, and to express how traumatic it was. I also felt so far removed from the ordinariness of my native English life.

Andrew, meanwhile, was starting to think more and more that South Sudan was too volatile for us to return there. The long-term effects on our family of what we had been through were not yet clear, but as we were all on edge, Andrew felt that we needed time to recover – in a place of peace. This was demonstrated one evening when Andrew and I found ourselves at an outdoor celebration. When the exuberant, sparkling fireworks were unleashed, instead of enjoying them as usual, I started to shake and sweat. My body reacted as if I were listening to gunfire, as if my children were unsafe, as if civil war was breaking out. While my mind was telling me that I was safe, I couldn't control my physical reaction. Thinking about our final evening in Juba still upset us many months later. Our youngest child was jumpy, clingy and tearful – he especially needed time to heal and feel secure again.

Despite all this, I initially battled Andrew's decision. We had committed to live and work in Juba for another year – once it was calm enough, shouldn't we just go back and fulfil our duty? I felt guilty at the thought of letting MAF down. Sometimes, though, the needs of a family outweigh duty.

One light, balmy summer evening, I sat at Esther's bedside in the beautiful London home of Juliet, who was generously hosting us. Our children found it alien trying to sleep when the sun was still up. Where they have grown up, near the equator, it is always dark around 7 p.m. and light around 7 a.m. The persistent summer sunshine of the northern hemisphere made sleep elusive. 'I just can't sleep!' Esther cried, despite lying in bed reading a storybook for a while.

After settling my daughter, I read from Proverbs 27 – and realised with a jolt that I needed to take advice from this book of ageless wisdom. 'Be sure you know the condition of your flocks,' verse 23 said. My flocks? I don't have flocks, but I do have children! It continued, 'give careful attention to your herds; for riches do not endure for ever'. My children were my riches, my responsibility – and everyone told me that they would grow up too fast, that the season of having them home would not endure forever. What if the needs, or condition, of my children right now required peace and stability, a school, and a mother who was less exhausted and tense?

What if these needs were greater right now than the need for us to return to South Sudan? I remembered that God is kind and how He had reassured me of His love and grace in Juba. I talked to God about the thoughts in my mind, then went downstairs to find Andrew. 'It's OK,' I told him. 'If you feel we need to leave Juba, I won't argue anymore.'

But even if we didn't return to South Sudan, we did not feel that it was time to break our link with Africa. We wanted to return to African soil because South Sudan, South Africa, Tanzania and Kenya were the homes our family knew. We also still felt passionate about the difference MAF could make to people living in remote corners of the earth. We were more than willing for Andrew to continue his work, if MAF still had a place for us.

We also recognised that our children needed closure. They missed their home. They asked about their friends. Joel especially was grieving for his friend Moses, whom he had left behind in tears on the day we evacuated. Joel had drawn a picture of himself asleep in his own bed at home in Juba. This is where he felt most secure, before all the changes – before the frightening disruption.

I knew without a doubt that my children needed to return to the continent they thought of as home. I also knew that, if possible, they needed to see our Juba home one last time, even if it was just to say goodbye.

Andrew informed MAF management of our decision. They graciously accepted our news, but the following months would be a period of waiting. Andrew would continue working for MAF South Sudan and would spend some time in Juba, but if there were no new openings, our contract would end by the start of 2017. In the meantime, MAF would send us as a family to live in Kenya until a decision could be made. And so we prepared to leave England, wondering where exactly our next home might be. We didn't have the answer, but thankfully God did.

45

A new placement

We discovered our next home just after midnight on 24 September 2016.

After a long flight from London and then a taxi from Nairobi's international airport, we stepped out, dishevelled, a weary little group. We stood bathed in the dim city glow of street lights while the concierge of Black Rose Apartments wiggled the key in the lock. The metal security gate clanked open, then the heavy wooden door was pushed back to reveal our new abode.

'Why is it so dark?' piped up a little voice.

'We're trying to turn the lights on,' answered Andrew, fumbling around near the door until a sudden burst of light illuminated a very orange apartment: orange walls, orange floors and orange tiles. Wow!

Despite its overpowering décor, our apartment at Black Rose was perfect provision. We heard a few days before our flight to Nairobi that this apartment had become available. It was just across the road from the MAF compound. Another MAF family, who came from Austria and were waiting to move to South Sudan for their first MAF placement, were staying in the same complex. This was great news. Kathie and Florian were already friends and their two girls got on well with our children. Instantly, our children had playmates on hand. The friendship of this family was a great blessing to us during our months at Black Rose.

Another blessing was that ours was the only apartment in the entire complex with its own washing machine – and the only apartment with three bedrooms. Thanks again to God's impeccable timing, we found ourselves in the one ground-floor flat that was large enough to absorb our family of five.

We settled in quickly. We didn't have much to unpack, since most of our goods were still in Juba. Andrew was soon back on duty. The crisis in South Sudan meant that more aid than ever was needed, so the pilots had a hectic schedule. Andrew spent a week up in Juba, then a week back with us in Nairobi. Each time he returned from Juba, he brought more items from our home, including our school resources. These were helpful as we tried to get into a new rhythm of homeschooling. Esther needed to work hard on her final year of primary school, Ben needed to buckle down with reading and maths, and Joel was just starting to learn letters and numbers. I despaired of how to spread myself across the varying needs of our children – but help was on its way.

Just up a flight of concrete stairs, Kathie was busy homeschooling her girls in their upstairs apartment. It was good to share the solidarity of homeschooling in our temporary situations. It also proved a great incentive for my children, since they knew they could hop outside to play with their friends if they worked hard and finished their assignments by early afternoon.

Soon, we heard that another couple were coming to stay at Black Rose Apartments for a temporary assignment. They were seasoned MAF staff who had worked for many years in Papua New Guinea. I looked at Kathie and joked, 'Imagine if the MAF lady moving here was a teacher and wanted to help us homeschool!' We smiled at the idea. It seemed too good to be true.

A few days later, the MAF couple arrived. There was a knock at our wooden front door and I opened it to meet Ruth, our new neighbour. She radiated kindness as she gently introduced herself. Ruth accepted my invitation to join me and Kathie for a cup of tea – but I nearly dropped the teacup when Ruth suddenly told us she had time on her hands and offered to help our families with homeschool, as she was an experienced teacher. I could barely believe my ears! What an incredible gift. Ruth became a much-loved friend to both me and my children and brought with her more proof of God's goodness in these months of transition. In fact, Ruth and her husband Larry were to be part of our MAF journey for many years to come.

That very same week, we received even more evidence of God's faithfulness. On Monday night, while Andrew was in Juba, I was asked to join him and our MAF UK managers on a three-way Skype meeting. The children were already asleep when I connected my laptop for the online call.

'Andrew and Liz,' one of the voices from England informed us, 'we would like to let you know that a pilot position has become available in Uganda. Is this a position you'd be interested in taking?'

We were thrilled! Andrew accepted for both of us – and a great peace settled over my heart. The huge pressure of uncertainty had just been lifted. We could continue our work with a mission group whose work we loved and believed in. We could remain in East Africa. Another thought instantly occurred to me: Uganda is the country I grew up hearing all about; where my mum invested two years of her life. It seemed amazing that, one generation later, her daughter – together with her son-in-law and grandchildren – would return to live and work in the land she loved and prayed for. How incredible that I would finally get to see the African country that had been such an inspiration to me so many years ago.

I knew I had to call Mum immediately. She listened to my excited babble of words. I waited for her reaction. She was quiet for a moment, before suddenly declaring, 'Oh, Liz! Oh! I can't believe it! I didn't even dare pray that MAF might have a position available in Uganda, in case it was just what *I* wanted and not what God wanted. I'm so happy to hear it!'

She was overwhelmed – and relieved for us that the uncertainty was over. Then she excitedly exclaimed, 'And I can come and visit!'

It was good news all round!

46

Final farewells to South Sudan

By mid-November, tensions had calmed in Juba. Certain NGOs and some MAF families had started to return. We asked our manager if we could go back to say our farewells before preparing for Uganda.

The answer was positive. It was safe enough for us to go back as a family and pack up our home. It was time to say goodbye, to remember the happy times – and put to rest some more difficult memories.

As Andrew was based in South Sudan that week, the children and I took a commercial flight out of Jomo Kenyatta airport in Nairobi one Monday morning. We would meet Andrew at our home in the evening.

While we were waiting at the airport, a staff member came to ask me if I had made a mistake. 'This is the departure gate for Juba,' he said. 'Are you perhaps waiting for the flight to Malindi?' He pointed over to the gate where relaxed holidaymakers were preparing for their flight to Kenya's stunning coast.

'No, this is definitely our flight,' I replied. He was taken aback.

Once on board the plane, one of the cabin crew bent down to speak with me discreetly before departure. 'Are you sure you're on the right flight with your children? This flight is for Juba...'

Yes, I reassured her, we fully intended to fly into Juba. All the Kenyan staff were concerned that I was taking young children into a city still reeling with the aftershock of fighting, which had caused many deaths and created a new wave of refugees. I appreciated their worry – but it also confirmed for me that taking our family to Uganda, a country that had been stable for many years, was a less volatile option after so much transition.

Our five days in Juba were a rollercoaster of action and emotion. Pushing open the glass front door and stepping into our house was a strange sensation. It was just the same, with our laundry where we had left it on the day we rushed off, toys littered across the floor, familiar books on the shelves – yet so much had changed in our lives. In the kitchen, there was evidence of Andrew passing through on his busy work days: a few dirty coffee cups, one or two items in the fridge. Other than that, an odd, abandoned air hung over the house. As I frantically packed over those next few days and our goods disappeared into boxes, this sense of abandonment grew.

On Thursday afternoon, Andrew returned from work early for an official farewell with the entire staff team – for both our family and another colleague who would not be returning to live in Juba. What a moving occasion. Once again, I was struck by the grace of the South Sudanese as they released us. One by one, South Sudanese colleagues stood up to speak, some bearing visible tribal scars on their foreheads and many bearing invisible scars ingrained by the years of war inflicted on their nation. 'This is painful for me,' one of them stated, as he spoke of the instability in their land. In the same breath, he told us that they understood why we were taking our children away, since their hopes of peace for South Sudan were not yet realised.

My heart ached for them. I looked at the many faces seated around us and knew that some had been through unimaginable difficulties in this war-torn land. I was sad to leave them, and so sad that we could not remain as an act of solidarity with our South Sudanese brothers and sisters.

The afternoon sun beat down overhead, but time stood still in our shady courtyard while staff members appreciated Andrew for his patience, for his calm manner, for never raising his voice, for the respectful way he interacted with staff. I sat in my plastic chair, the familiar sweaty sheen forming on my face and neck, but a smile on my face. The kind words spoken over Andrew made me feel honoured to be his wife. His colleagues were going to miss him – and I knew Andrew would very much miss them too, as well as flying in South Sudan. In all his MAF years, the work he carried out there stands out as the most fulfilling. It was a small consolation that he would still fly in and out of South Sudan from Uganda – but it wouldn't be the same.

Both Andrew and I stood in turn to appreciate our colleagues and reassure them that although we were leaving, we would not forget them. After all the speeches, we called the children over. They were joyfully sticky from sugar and their faces shiny from sweat. They had been running about in the heat with armfuls of sweet treats they had taken from a table nearby that was laid out with food for the farewell. No matter, we were all gathered up in a loving circle of prayer as God's kindness and peace were prayed over us. This generous act of grace reminded me of a similar circle: when we stood on the Dodoma airstrip almost three years earlier and were released from Tanzania. How blessed we had been to live and work in two such loving communities.

This was not our only farewell. That final week in Juba, many of our non-MAF friends were in town. It was wonderful to see once more friends from our church, from other organisations, Joel's teacher and our South Sudanese pastor. One humid evening, a MAF and non-MAF group joined together for an early dinner in the front courtyard of Quality Hotel. By meeting there, we replaced a dark memory with a lighter memory. This time, we got our meal and everything was calm. However, it felt somehow unreal, so different from our life there before evacuation. Many of our MAF team were still back in Kenya. We were also aware that this gathering would be short-lived: the sorrow of goodbye hung in the air around us.

My only regret that week was that I did not get to see Grace, but I was reassured by speaking to her on the phone and loved hearing her voice. For me, one of the hardest aspects of our evacuation was not knowing how everyone else was when we departed so suddenly; our community was so abruptly scattered. I worried about Grace, our colleagues, our church friends and acquaintances from the wider community. Now the anxieties that plagued me were being put to rest as we spoke to or met up with several of these people during our week in Juba. It was a solace. We were being given the gift of 'goodbye' – the gift of closure.

I repeatedly experienced God's same compassion when He caused many of the people I cared about and knew from Juba to cross my path during the months following our evacuation. We lost contact with many people when fighting broke out. Chaos caused the mobile phone network to crash; other people lost phones or changed to Kenyan or Ugandan numbers as they crossed the borders into neighbouring countries. Yet incredibly God allowed me to unexpectedly run in to Juba friends all over the enormous city of Nairobi: in shopping centres, at restaurants, in car parks and at markets. Each time, another little crack in my hurting heart was healed as I witnessed how God had answered our prayers and kept these people safe.

There was one more task I needed to face in Juba during that final week of packing up: a task I had been dreading. Bracing myself one morning, I set off from our front door to retrace my steps towards the homeschool room. With every step, emotion threatened as I recalled the stressful day we left. Turning the key in the schoolroom lock, a rush of memories cascaded into my mind. I pulled open the door and looked in at a scene exactly as I had left it on 9 July. Even the calendar was still open at July, with events marked for later in the month that never happened. Work to do was laid out on the desks and my carefully organised lesson plans lay unfulfilled. Now my emotions were spilling over. So much time and effort, passion and love had gone into making this place work as our 'school' – making it possible for us to be in South Sudan with Andrew. Here, my children and I had argued, laughed, cried and created together.

Tearing down the children's work seemed harsh, but I was under pressure. I had just one day to empty this room, to decide what to throw away, what to give away and what to pack for Uganda. I popped my head around the door to call for the children, asking them to come and see their schoolroom before I started dismantling everything inside. I wanted them to remember it as it had been before evacuation. In they trooped, my noisy brood, bringing Joel's special South Sudanese friend with them. The two boys were delighted to be reunited and to have this week together.

The children looked around. Esther and Ben posed for a photo by their desks, happy to be back, but equally happy that today was not a school day. I asked Joel if he wanted to be in a photo too. His face dropped and the blue of his eyes misted over with tears. He shook his head vehemently. 'It's too sad,' he mumbled.

I knew exactly what he meant. I cried as I took down each picture, each piece of work, each poster. We hadn't expected it to end so abruptly. So much of my life in Juba had been taken up with schooling the children; it seemed almost sacrilegious to tear it apart so hastily.

By Friday lunchtime, we were all crying as we took a final look at the compound which had been home for two short, but intense, years. Today we were leaving Juba for good. Esther felt the wrench deeply, her head aching from crying. She was losing friends, a home and a country all over again. At ten years old, she had already lived in five countries. She needed to grieve this latest loss. I felt so sad for her. I fished in my bag for Calpol (children's paracetamol) and a bottle of water to ease her discomfort and prayed silently but fervently that our next home would give my daughter a longer period of stability.

Andrew had a busy work day and had departed at dawn to set off on his flights. We would see him back in Kenya. Esther, Ben, Joel and I made our way out of the front door and along the path to the car park, pulling our cases behind us and waving a final goodbye to our home. We climbed into the MAF vehicle taking us to the airport. I was suddenly exhausted with the emotion, the goodbyes, the physical effort of speed packing. Our ever-smiling South Sudanese colleague John accompanied us across town, on a drive without drama, without checkpoints. Wrapped in the humidity of Juba heat, we made our way through the now bustling airport one last time and prepared for our return to Nairobi on an impersonal commercial aeroplane. In just a few more weeks, we would pack up our temporary Nairobi home and turn our eyes towards a new home, a new country, a new start.

As our plane taxied up the runway, we strained for our last peek at the land which had come to mean so much to us. A land which sent me away richer in faith, richer in friendships, richer in understanding the faithfulness of a God who is bigger than war, bigger than hospital horror stories, bigger than trauma and bigger than my failures and fears. I recalled the question Margaret had asked me, back in Dodoma: 'Liz, is your God big enough?' As our plane started to speed up for take-off, I knew without a doubt the answer: YES! He is more than big enough to handle all this – and more.

I had with me a card a dear American friend had handed me when we caught up with each other that week. She had evacuated from Juba a few days after us and had experienced far more threatening incidents. Inside her card, this courageous friend had written the words from a song our Juba church loved to sing: 'Our God is greater'. Not only was God big enough to trust in the midst of the unknown, in civil unrest, in sorrow, in poverty, but He was greater than I could ever comprehend or imagine. He would continue to care for His people in South Sudan. He would continue to guide my family as we moved further south down the vast African continent and into Uganda.

I tucked her card safely into my bag, then pulled out my phone and took a final photo from the window as the plane banked over deep, green swampland. The mighty River Nile was slowly disappearing into the background and all too soon the city of Juba was fading into a memory.

Goodbye, South Sudan. Thank you for the lessons learnt, for the evidence of God's faithful promises kept over and over again, for the colleagues who loved and then released us so graciously. You will always have a piece of my heart; you will forever remain in my prayers.

Part Six

Uganda

DECEMBER 2016 ONWARDS

47

A spacious place – our new home

The taxi drew up at the bottom of a steep slope, guarded by enormous double gates. The taxi driver hooted once, twice, then a short, wiry young man swung the gates open. Accelerating, the taxi began the ascent up the slope in front of us. I glanced back at the man, our new guard for our new house. Esther, Ben and Joel were craning their necks and elbowing one another across the seats in their enthusiasm to get their first glimpse of our new home in Uganda.

The car came to a halt in front of a long, rectangular, single-storey house, perched at the top of the steep driveway. A green, sloping garden wrapped itself around the property. Tall trees, bushes and plants around the perimeter nodded their healthy leaves at us. The children tumbled out of the taxi with great exclamations of excitement and were already running across the grass, keen to explore every corner of their new garden. Andrew's long legs emerged from the vehicle's front passenger door. He unfolded himself to his full height and strode towards a solid metal door at the nearest end of the house. Passing under a wooden awning, he untangled a bunch of keys, then pulled the metal door open. 'Welcome to our new home,' he said, grinning at me.

I smiled broadly and followed him across the tarmac parking area to the house. We pushed open a netted fly-screen door and stepped into the kitchen. A basket of welcoming goodies had been thoughtfully placed on top of the wooden counter. I gratefully spied a box of teabags and an ice cream container that seemed to have cake inside. Taking a few more steps, we wandered into a wide lounge with a polished wooden floor. I turned slightly to my right and was greeted by a whole wall of windows offering incredible hillside views over Kampala, Uganda's capital city. There was a generous veranda just beyond the windows where we could sit outside and admire this astonishing view.

I loved this house immediately – but the sense of space and the view were not the most striking features of our arrival. Across the lounge walls, someone had suspended a banner. In bold, colourful, hand-written letters we read, 'WELCOME HOME, LIZ, ANDREW, ESTHER, BEN, JOEL.' My eyes filled with thankful tears. In Juba, when circumstances threatened to overwhelm me, I had cried into my pillow and pleaded with God for a new home, a place of peace. Now I felt like that prayer had been answered. We had entered a different season – and I felt the warmth of a Heavenly Father's undeserved kindness encircle me like a comforting hug.

I later discovered that the welcome banner had been made and sent from the UK by Wendy and her family – the same friend who helped me welcome Joel into the world almost six years earlier. Her thoughtfulness meant the world to us. The banner gave us confidence that we were loved, even as we started again in our fifth African country and were yet to make friends.

We had only been in our new house a matter of minutes when the young guard, Amani, came to the door and called for us. We had guests! These were special guests: Joel's close friend Moses from Juba and his parents, who were visiting Kampala. Knowing they had to return to South Sudan shortly, we had made a date for the very afternoon of our arrival. It was a fun tea party. He and Joel, Esther and Ben were delighted to have time together. Andrew and I were equally delighted to share a cup of tea with familiar friends in this unfamiliar city. It somehow provided a bridge between our old home and our new one.

Twelve days after arriving in Uganda, we celebrated Christmas quietly, feeling very new and a little lonely – but just a few days later, the gates swung open again for more guests. This time, Nathalie and her family visited us, having arrived from northern Uganda, where they had settled with YWAM. We hadn't seen them since the tense morning of our evacuation from Juba. It had been stressful not knowing when and where we would meet again, but five months later, the reunion was about to happen! We could celebrate that we had all ended up in the same country, albeit several hours away by road.

I rushed outdoors, anxious to meet Nathalie and her family again. Thank goodness that the French are not intimidated by shows of emotion because as I threw my arms around my friend, happy tears ran unchecked down my face. The children connected easily despite the months apart. Nathalie's son was full of enthusiasm as he described to Andrew their evacuation from Juba in a military aircraft. Once again, I sensed the goodness of God as He allowed us not only to meet up again, but to continue our connection in Uganda.

Several months later, we received more surprising news. Nadia's family were moving to Kampala and would live down the road from our home! When I left South Sudan, I noted in my journal that two of the greatest treasures from my time there were my friendships with Nadia and Nathalie. Now both of these precious friends had, like us, been gathered out of Juba and placed in Uganda. After all the years of moving countries, of sorrow-filled farewells and of starting friendships over and over, I had been granted extra time with two close friends.

I thanked God sincerely for this unprecedented gift. For the next two years, Nadia and her family were nearby. This was also a bonus for Joel, who now had a familiar friend from Juba: Nadia's daughter, Eliyah. They had been at preschool together and had spent many busy hours playing outdoors on the Juba compound. Both Nadia and I were pleased when Joel and Eliyah joined the same class at their new Kampala school. Joel had struggled the most with our recent transitions, so having a playmate he knew from before Kampala eased the differences between South Sudan and Uganda. There was yet another joy in store when we received news that good friends Ruth and Larry would be moving from Nairobi to Uganda as well.

Andrew slipped easily into his work routine with his new team. He especially loved the days that his MAF flights took him over the border and back into South Sudan. He and I were thankful that he was still 'flying planes for God in Africa' and working for MAF.

All three of our children enrolled at Kampala's Heritage International School. When I dropped each of them off at their respective classrooms, I remembered how I prayed in Juba one Sunday morning for the Lord to 'make a way' for Esther to go to school and yet live at home. Leaving Juba so suddenly was sad for us all, but I could now see how God could use even this for good, making a way for something new. In just a few short months, Esther would join the secondary school and would still be living at home.

As I left the children at school and drove home, I was unsure what to do with the time I suddenly had on my hands. In Juba, every day felt like a battle to keep my head above water – life was so busy. Trying to juggle my different roles and coping with tense security situations left me exhausted. Kampala was the opposite.

'I'm like a bouncy ball!' I told a friend. 'I can't settle down, I can't sit still. I bounce from one thing to the next, but have nothing really to do – it feels so wrong.'

One Tuesday morning, soon after moving to Kampala, I felt overcome with anxiety as my body tried to adapt to this new, slower life. My heart rate increased and I had chest pains. Thinking I was unwell, I decided to drive to the doctor's surgery with a MAF neighbour. The experienced doctor looked kindly at me then asked, 'Have you come out of a stressful event recently?' When I tried to explain about Juba, I became tearful.

Later, a concerned MAF staff member gently asked if I would have some counselling. I attended three sessions with a helpful counsellor who gave me strategies to manage the feelings of panic which had accompanied me out of Juba – with the evening at Quality Hotel, the evacuation, the death of the men in the street and the shooting of our neighbouring shopkeeper. Having so much time meant that I was starting to process the more challenging events of our two years in South Sudan. It was a natural process of winding down.

'Kampala is a healing place,' a kind-hearted new friend told me, after I confided some of the emotional struggles we were experiencing as we adapted to a calmer environment. I trusted her judgement. She too knew what it was to evacuate from a country not her own when fighting broke out, although her experience had been in a different African nation.

In the mornings, after the children had left for school, I loved to spend time with my best friend, Jesus. One morning, as I turned to Psalm 18, the words in front of me surprised me, then made me smile as I realised that the healing process had already commenced:

> *He reached down from on high and took hold of me;*
> *he drew me out of deep waters…*
> *He brought me out into a spacious place;*
> *he rescued me because he delighted in me.*
>
> (Verses 16 and 19)

The words perfectly summed up my recent experience. God had definitely taken hold of me and drawn me out of the deep waters of feeling overwhelmed. He had told me that He delighted in me. He had rescued our team and our friends from the dark threat of civil war.

I walked across to the wide-open doors of our lounge and stepped outside on to the veranda, taking in the bright red flowers in the flowerbed next to me, the verdant sweep of our garden and the stunning view of Kampala's tree-studded city below. There was so much light – so much space. God had done exactly as His word said – He had brought me out to 'a spacious place'. I thanked Him as I stood in that spacious place right now. Our way-making, promise-keeping God had again faithfully acted according to His word.

48

A full circle

Eight months after our arrival in Uganda, my mum did exactly what she had hoped. She came to visit – and brought my dad for his first visit to the country she had told him so much about.

She was excited to be back on Ugandan soil and be with her daughter's family, glimpsing their life in a country she held so dear and seeing her grandchildren. Her joy bubbled up inside her, her happiness fizzing over and bursting out as she emerged from the arrivals hall into the warmth of Entebbe airport.

I ran to greet my beloved parents, my children right behind me, tripping over themselves in their eagerness to welcome their grandparents to their new home. Huge smiles, a flurry of hugs. Our enthusiastic children practically dragged Nana and Grandad to our waiting car.

After almost fifty years of marriage, Dad was finally seeing the land where Mum had ventured before becoming his bride. He had a wide-eyed wonder as he surveyed the bustle of the airport, then the long, busy stretch of Entebbe Road on our drive home to Kampala. Gazing out of the window, he took in the activity alongside the main road. Men frying *rolex*, a Ugandan street food, the oily smoke enveloping the vendors as they worked. Metalworkers bent over their creations, white-hot sparks adding to the heat of the Ugandan afternoon. Chickens pecking furiously at the dusty ground, vegetables laid out on wooden tables and stray dogs lying lazily between the food stalls. Women, men and children everywhere he looked, the colours of their clothes vivid in the sunlight. People busy making, busy selling, busy buying.

This was modern-day city life – a world away from the images projected by mum's black-and-white slides that we watched together years ago. Photographs of remote Kotido, snapped half a century earlier, presented a very different perception of Uganda. Would my parents be able to capture anything of 1960s Kotido on this visit?

The answer came just over a week later. Andrew was booked to fly passengers from a Catholic mission group and from Food for the Hungry. The flight not only required a stop at Kotido airstrip, but there happened to be enough spare seats on the flight for Mum, Dad – and me. Our sense of anticipation grew as we looked forward to Monday 7 August 2017 – almost exactly fifty years since

Mum stepped off her flight from London and first set foot on Ugandan soil.

We departed before dawn had had a chance to pierce the lingering darkness. Dropping the children off with friends, we continued our drive to Kajansi airfield, the MAF Uganda base. On our arrival, Andrew disappeared, busily on duty. Preflighting a plane takes time, so I took my parents to wait in the ticket hall. They were delighted to be given a very British cup of tea.

When our MAF flight was called, we made our way across the misty airfield, still glistening with dew, the birdsong jubilant. Kajansi airfield, which borders the magnificent Lake Victoria, is one of the most beautiful ones I know. Tall, green rushes swayed gently in the breeze, separating the lake from the airfield. The awakening morning sunlight glinted on the glass of the cockpit windscreen and highlighted the red and blue colours of the MAF plane.

'How do you feel, Mum?' I asked, as we approached the plane which would take her back to the place she once called home.

'I can't really believe it,' she began. 'To fly over Uganda after all these years – with my own son-in-law as pilot!'

There were two seats available right behind the pilot, so my parents settled themselves there. Andrew passed them his aerial maps of Uganda and I seized the moment to photograph Mum pointing out some of the routes she had travelled, when a journey from Kampala to Kotido was a whole day's drive, over potholed roads. In a MAF plane, we would be in Kotido in less than two hours, even with a brief stop at Moroto for one passenger to alight. We took off swiftly and when we stopped at Moroto a short while later, Andrew took the opportunity to invite Mum into the cockpit.

So it was that my mum once more got her first sightings of her much-loved Kotido from the co-pilot seat of a MAF plane. The plane swooped low, the vast Karamoja region spread out for miles beneath us. As soon as she spied the sandy ground and familiar village settlements, she felt her heart rate quicken and the pricking of tears behind her eyes. The closer we flew to Kotido, the more vivid the memories became.

'I've never seen it so green!' Mum yelled over the engine noise, surprised by the colour of a land she remembered as a dusty, semi-arid wilderness, baked brown by a harsh sun.

'We've had an unusual amount of rain this year,' shouted back Andrew.

When the plane dropped closer to the ground, a young boy, dressed simply in a dark piece of material, darted across the airstrip. He threw rocks at his cows so that they moved hastily off the dirt airstrip – and Andrew brought the plane down to a safe landing.

Mum was suddenly very quiet. The engine stopped and the door was pulled open. The airstrip was even quieter. This was rural, remote Karamoja – a world away from bustling towns and cities. A small group of curious children gathered silently around the plane, watching to see who would emerge. Likewise, I looked at my mum, keen to see her reaction as she began to make her way down the metal steps. After setting her feet on the rocky ground, she immediately extended her hand towards one of the boys, who was clad like his friend in a simple cloth tossed over his shoulder and wound around his body. A ring of black, blue and yellow beads and a pair of rubber sandals strapped over his dusty feet were his only other adornment. Like the other boys, he carried a thin, wooden rod to drive the cattle or goats.

Mum was visibly moved as their hands joined together. Here was a lady in her seventies from a distant culture clasping the hand of a boy not older than ten: his skin dark, her skin light. His world was overlooked by a persistent African sun and filled with tasks that revolved around a pastoral lifestyle. Her world was overlooked by inconstant British weather and filled with a ceaseless round of activity, gadgets and a legacy of educating the younger generations. It might appear that they had nothing in common. Yet in that moment, the years and the miles separating the two cultures they represented ceased to matter. My mum was connecting with a people group she loved, had never forgotten and who had remained in her prayers for more than fifty years. Mum's emotions overflowed and, although her happy smile was intact, her tears were unstoppable. The boy smiled back.

Hearing a sniffle behind me, I looked back and saw that my dad was fighting back his emotions as he watched the scene unfold. 'Oh, Dad,' I said, fondly. 'Don't you cry too, or they'll be no stopping any of us!' I dabbed a tissue to my own eyes.

There was no holding my mum back after that. She moved across to meet the other children standing nearby, similarly dressed and equipped, some with earrings. Smiling, she shook hands all round. Next, she tried to recall her Karamojong greetings, but was apparently rather rusty, judging from the shrieks of laughter which met her efforts. '*Awah! Awah!*' we heard, as their amusement rang out. A semicircle of children gathered naturally around her as she grinned at them and tried to make herself understood – but communication was challenging.

Suddenly inspired, she launched into a rendition of a song she used to sing with her students under a tamarind tree, perhaps somewhere not too far from where she stood now. That was an age ago and the sound of those happy voices had long since faded away; now she could only remember one song in Karamojong: the old Sunday School chorus 'Zacchaeus was a very little man...' The children roared with laughter – and I couldn't help laughing too. They were fascinated by this foreign lady's attempts to engage with them. While they may not have understood what she was trying to say, I hope these curious onlookers understood that she liked them and wanted to communicate that they mattered to her – just as her students and the community where she lived and worked mattered deeply to her fifty years earlier.

Her students at Kotido Girls' School had known instinctively that their teacher from far-off England loved them and was driven by a passion to see her students thrive: the motivating force of all good teachers. They felt the value of her heartfelt prayers as she prayed for and with them. The fact that some shared her faith gives Mum even greater comfort than their academic achievements because she knows that this is an eternal legacy she passed on. A few kept in touch after Mum left Uganda, despite the difficulties of communicating long-distance and the troubles Uganda faced under Idi Amin's tyrannical rule. Sadly, some have since died.

Back in 1969, Mum's heart felt like it was breaking as she climbed into a car that would take her away from all that had become so dear. She thought she would never see any of those schoolgirls ever again – but she was wrong.

Mum was thrilled when one of her students came to visit her home in Lancashire many years later. Anna Grace Okia arrived accompanied by one of her four daughters, who had married a British man, and her grandchildren. While visiting her family in the UK, Anna Grace Okia also wanted to visit her teacher from years before.

In her own words, Mum wrote,

That was an amazing experience and came out of the blue. Anna Grace Okia had helped me in my house to earn her school fees which I then paid... She helped with various tasks such as washing, ironing, cleaning and interpreting when village ladies came to sell their wood. She also heated up water on the fire for my daily bath and filled my tin bathtub.

It was overwhelming to meet her again after so many years. She had been a keen Christian and a brilliant student. I used to tell her how much cleverer she was than I would ever be. She obtained a place at a CMS secondary school in Kampala (very few girls were able to gain a secondary education in those days), went on to qualify as a teacher, married a headmaster of a boy's school (who was later killed by Idi Amin's soldiers) and then returned to Karamoja to oversee girls' education.

Anna Grace Okia had not been well when she made the visit to see Mum. A short while later, Mum received the unhappy news that this student who she had been so proud of, and so glad to see again, had passed away. My brother Ian kindly drove Mum to the funeral in Nottingham, where she was moved to see Anna Grace's family again and a handful of mutual friends who had been in Kotido during the years Mum taught there.

God had granted Mum a meaningful gift in meeting Anna Grace Okia in England – and one she had never imagined possible. How encouraging it was to hear that this excellent student had used her skills and knowledge to continue the investment in girls' education in Karamoja.

Back on the airstrip in Kotido, Andrew was starting to round up his passengers but first, I aimed the camera lens at the group of Karamojong children with my mum. A picture of my mother with her past in Kotido lit up the camera screen. I had captured a tangible memory of this unique moment.

Next, I lined my parents up in front of the MAF plane, the dusty stretch of Karamoja panning out behind. Before I could press the shutter, one of the MAF passengers stepped forward. 'This is such a great story! Let me take a photograph of all of you,' she offered.

The camera lens clicked again. We thanked our photographer and I glanced at the new image. Now I saw my mother captured with a present-day link to Uganda: her son-in-law, her daughter and a MAF plane.

Mum was reluctant to leave. The children accompanied her to the open door and watched patiently while she found a seat behind my dad, who had been promoted to the co-pilot's seat. As the engine started to hum, they scampered away from the plane but lined up at the edge of the airstrip, still curious. Mum lifted her hand to wave through the window as Andrew positioned us for take-off. The children waved back. The engine gained power and the plane sped up, gliding smoothly into the skies above Kotido. Gradually, the plane carried my mum up and over her beloved Kotido. The children became distant, tiny dots far below. The airstrip became an insignificant slice of brown in the huge, open landscape. For the second time, Ann was being carried away from Kotido. The tears slid silently down her cheeks.

As Andrew set the plane on course for Moyo, my dad leaned forward to marvel at the views stretched below, the huge sweep of grasslands. I looked across at Mum. Her eyes were red – I passed her another tissue.

'Mum, are you OK?'

She nodded, crying and laughing at the same time. A rainbow smile.

'Oh, Liz, it's amazing! But I'm so sad to leave again – it reminds me of leaving the first time. And why are those boys still herding cattle? It's just like it was when I lived there so many years ago. That's so sad to see. I'm going to redouble my prayers for Karamoja.'

She had never stopped praying – never stopped carrying the people of Karamoja in her heart. She had hoped to see more change and progress in this often neglected region of Uganda. Disappointment weighed heavy on her teacher's heart.

'Are you glad you came today, Mum?' I prompted her, knowing full well that she was but wanting to hear the sweet side of a bittersweet visit.

Over the roar of our plane's engine, she leaned across to continue our conversation. 'Oh yes! I'm so, so glad I got to come to Kotido – and on a MAF plane with Andrew as the pilot! It's so incredible. I never, ever imagined that I would come back – especially like this! I'm glad you and Dad have seen Kotido too. What a *wonderful* blessing this day is!'

I, too, was glad. What an incredible privilege to get a glimpse into my mother's history and the place God called her to all those years ago. And now here we were, soaring over the same land, my husband in his MAF uniform, doing the work he had been called to do: 'flying planes for God in Africa'. We never could have imagined our life either. If it was written as a fictional story, it would seem too perfectly crafted – this full circle; this story of a faithful God who has cared for us every step of the way. As Mum recently said, when asked about the trip, 'When our little daughter Liz was born, we never in our wildest dreams imagined that she would one day grow up to marry a MAF pilot and eventually serve with him in Uganda.'

And not just in Uganda, but in Tanzania, South Sudan and Kenya – and with four years of preparation in South Africa. Through each incredible country, through every up and down, through the inspiring people we have met along the way and the stories of those who have been changed by God's love, there has been one constant: the presence of our promise-keeping God. His faithfulness, plan, compassion and love go further than the MAF planes, further than our journey – and further than our wildest dreams.

Now to him who is able to do immeasurably more than all we ask or imagine, according to his power that is at work within us, to him be glory in the church and in Christ Jesus throughout all generations, for ever and ever! Amen.
(Ephesians 3:20–21)

DISCOVERY AIR PASS

MAF

SEE MORE OF THE WORLD WITH MAF

FIND OUT WHERE YOUR AIR PASS WILL TAKE YOU...

PAPUA NEW GUINEA

SOUTH SUDAN
YOUR FIRST EXCITING DESTINATION

Ever wondered what it's like to live, work and serve in some of the most isolated places on earth?

Join us on a journey of discovery to visit places rarely featured in travel brochures, and to meet people living far from the tourist trail.

Every couple of months, you will receive a new country pass by post or email: updates from our pilots, real-life stories and interesting country facts you can't read anywhere else!

To get your free Discovery Air Pass, scan the QR code or visit the website below

ving for Life

www.maf-uk.org/lizparker

Registered charity in England and Wales (1064598) and in Scotland (SC039107)
® Registered trademark 3026860, 3026908, 3026915